W9-AYU-806

THE ATLAS AND
           TITAN MISSILES

URANIUM

THE COSMOS

CHAOS

AN ACHILLES' HEEL

EUROPE

A TROJAN HORSE

Behind these words are exciting and engrossing tales—of gods and men, of heroic exploits and tragedy, of strength and frailty, of worlds created and cities destroyed, all given shape by one of the greatest flowerings of the imagination humanity has ever known.

To read *Words from the Myths* is to enter into a dazzling voyage of discovery of the glory that was Greece—and the enduring wonder and magic of language.

"Scholarly . . . yet reads easily. A boon for the curious mind"—*Commonweal*

"A succinct retelling of Greek myths . . . a demonstration of their contribution to everyday and scientific language"—*Saturday Review*

ISAAC ASIMOV was born in the USSR in 1920, but was brought up in Brooklyn, N.Y. Currently a faculty member of Boston University School of Medicine, he is the author of nearly 100 books, ranging from science fiction novels to scholarly works on mathematics and mythology.

Other MENTOR Books of Special Interest

☐ **MYTHOLOGY by Edith Hamilton.** A brilliant retelling of the classic Greek, Roman, and Norse legends of love and adventure, by the author of **The Greek Way.** (#MW1354—$1.50)

☐ **THE ANCIENT MYTHS by Norma Lorre Goodrich.** A vivid recounting of the great myths of Greece, Egypt, India, Persia, Crete, Sumer, and Rome. (#MQ1012—95¢)

☐ **MYTHS OF THE GREEKS AND ROMANS by Michael Grant.** The world's great myths and their impact on creative arts through the ages. (#MJ1336—$1.95)

☐ **GODS, HEROES, AND MEN OF ANCIENT GREECE by W. H. D. Rouse.** The timeless tales of the superhuman men and all-too-human gods of ancient Greek mythology, retold with gusto and humor in a modern version. (#MY1299—$1.25)

ISAAC ASIMOV

WORDS FROM THE MYTHS

Decorations by WILLIAM BARSS

A SIGNET BOOK from
NEW AMERICAN LIBRARY
TIMES MIRROR

SIGNET TRADEMARK REG. U.S. PAT. OFF. AND FOREIGN COUNTRIES
REGISTERED TRADEMARK—MARCA REGISTRADA
HECHO EN CHICAGO, U.S.A.

SIGNET, SIGNET CLASSICS, MENTOR, PLUME AND MERIDIAN
BOOKS *are published by The New American Library, Inc.,
1301 Avenue of the Americas, New York, New York 10019*

FIRST PRINTING, SEPTEMBER, 1969

    4 5 6 7 8 9 10 11 12

PRINTED IN THE UNITED STATES OF AMERICA

To Austin Olney

CONTENTS

INTRODUCTION

HUMAN BEINGS wouldn't be human if they didn't wonder about the world about them. Many thousands of years ago, when mankind was still primitive, men must have looked out of caves and wondered about what they saw. What made the lightning flash? Where did the wind come from? Why would winter start soon and why would all the green things die? And then why did they all come back to life the next spring?

Man wondered about himself, too. Why did men get sick sometimes? Why did all men get old and die eventually? Who first taught men how to use fire and how to weave cloth?

There were any number of questions but there were no answers. These were the days before science; before men had learned to experiment in order to determine the hows and whys of the universe.

What early man had to do was to invent what seemed to be the most logical answers. The raging wind was like the blowing of an angry man. The wind, however, was much stronger than the breath of any ordinary man and it had been blowing ever since man could remember. Therefore, the wind must be created by a tremendously huge and powerful man, one who never died. Such a superhuman being was a "god" or "demon."

The lightning seemed, perhaps, the huge, deadly spear of another god. Then, since arrows killed men, disease could be the result of invisible arrows fired by still another god.

Since men and women married and had children, perhaps the green plants of the world were the children of the sky (a god) and the earth (a goddess). The gentle rain which made the plants grow was the marriage between them.

Perhaps a goddess was in charge of the plants of the world and grew angry because of some misfortune. She might have refused to let plants grow until things had been straightened out. That was why the green things died and winter came and that's why the world grew green again when winter was over and spring came.

Every group of human beings made up such stories; and some groups were more interesting and clever at it than others. Foremost in excellence were the ancient Greeks. They were a lively, imaginative people with great literary talents, and they made up some of the most fascinating tales of this sort. They called such stories "mythos" which is a Greek word that simply means "tale" or "story." We use the word "myth" nowadays to mean a particular kind of story; one which contains fanciful or supernatural incidents intended to explain nature, or one which deals with the gods and demons that were invented by early man.

The Greeks took their myths very seriously. Since the gods controlled natural forces, it was wise to treat them with careful consideration. They had to be bribed to send rain when it was needed, and pleaded with not to send disease or misfortune. For that reason, animals were sacrificed to them, beautiful temples were built for them, songs were composed to praise them. Thus, a religion grew up about the myths.

For over a thousand years, the people of the ancient world (from whom we inherit our civilization) believed in this religion. The great literature which they produced was filled with it. They named the stars and planets after characters in the myths. They told stories of dimly remembered ancestors whom they made the sons of the various gods and goddesses. They named their children after these god-descended "heroes."

After Christianity was established, the old religion died out and Europeans no longer believed in the old Greek and Roman gods. Those gods and the myths about them lived on in memory, however. The old literature did not die; it was too great to be allowed to die. We read Homer's *Iliad* and *Odyssey* even today. We read the great plays written by the Greek dramatists. We read Aesop's fables and the historical and philosophical works of the Greeks and Romans. All are full of the gods and the myths.

In fact, the old Greek stories were so fascinating that even after Christianity was established, men did not consider themselves really educated unless and until they had learned those stories. Educated men introduced words from the myths into their speaking and some of those words remained in the language. For that reason, traces of the Greek myths are to be found today in every European tongue, including English.

For instance, a police car's signal is a siren and a sea cow is a sirenian. A circus organ is a calliope; a jelly-fish is a medusa; and an Australian anteater is an echidna. We call out in a stentorian voice; listen to a kindly mentor or a bearded nestor; despise a hectoring bully.

In every case mentioned, we are drawing upon the Greek stories, where a Siren was a death trap, Calliope a goddess, Medusa and Echidna horrible monsters, and Stentor, Mentor, Nestor, and Hector were men.

Scientists, particularly, drew upon the old myths. Until quite recently, Latin and Greek were the common languages of learned men of all nations. When some new animal or planet or chemical or phenomenon needed to be named, it would have been inconvenient if scientists of each nationality used names drawn from their own language. The habit arose of giving a Latin or Greek name which all nationalities could use.

Since the Greek myths are so well known it was natural to take words from those myths whenever they seemed to fit the situation. For instance, when uranium was first being broken down by fission during World War II, a new element was found amid the deadly radioactive heat. It was named "promethium" after Prometheus, a character in the Greek myths who dared the deadly radioactive heat of the sun to bring fire to mankind.

Most of us are introduced to Greek myths in childhood but are taught to think of them only as interesting fairy tales and adventure stories. However, as you see, they are more than that. They are part of our culture, and much of our language, particularly our scientific language, is derived from them.

What I would like to do, then, in this book, is to go over some of the Greek myths once again and see how they gave rise to words and expressions we use today. I want to show the manner in which these old, old stories, which have been living now for three thousand years, still penetrate our daily lives. By understanding the myths, we will understand ourselves better.

For instance, let's begin, as the Greeks did, with the beginning.

1 THE BEGINNING

THE GREEKS imagined that, to begin with, the universe was composed of completely mixed and confused matter. Nothing had any particular shape or form. The universe was merely a raw material out of which nothing had yet been made. The Greeks called this raw material *Chaos*.

The word "chaos" means, in Greek, an open gulf. The word "chasm," which means that also, comes from the same root as does chaos. The original chaos can be pictured, then, as something like outer space, but with none of the stars and planets formed yet. Everything existed merely as a kind of swirling and transparent vapor. Only emptiness, only a vast open gulf, would then seem to exist. (Actually, modern scientists think that is how the universe really did exist to begin with.)

We still use the word "chaos" today to express anything that is in hopeless confusion and disorder, even if it's just a room with its contents scattered all about.

The word has come down to us in another and more

familiar form, but one which is practically never recognized.

About 1600, a Flemish chemist named Jan Baptista van Helmont was studying the vapors that were produced when charcoal was burned. He was interested also in the airlike bubbles formed when fruit juice was allowed to stand.

These vapors and different kinds of "airs" were not like the ordinary liquids and solids that chemists deal with. A vapor has no shape of its own. When it is inside a container, the container seems empty. Such a substance, without shape or form, is an example of chaos. Van Helmont decided to use a name for it that was suggested by the word. His language was Flemish (a dialect of Dutch) and he spelled "chaos" according to the Flemish pronunciation —"gas."

Now the fuel that is used in automobiles today is liquid as it is pumped into the fuel tank. In the engine, however, it vaporizes and turns into a gas. It is only a gas that can combine with air to drive the pistons and run the engine. Because the liquid turns into gas so easily, it is named "gasoline." Americans usually call it "gas" for short.

So when we "step on the gas" we are using a word that traces all the way back to the Greek word for the original state of the universe. And when, during a morning rush hour, too many motorists are stepping on the gas at the same time, the result is chaos indeed.

When things with form and shape were created out of Chaos, the result was *Cosmos*. This is a Greek word meaning "order" and "good arrangement" and is therefore just the opposite of Chaos. It is quite common, nowadays, to refer to the universe as the "cosmos." The word comes into play in other ways, too.

For instance, in 1911, a new type of radiation was discovered, which seemed to be bombarding the earth from all sides. The radiation seemed to be coming from everywhere in the universe, from the whole cosmos, in fact. Therefore, the American physicist Robert A. Millikan suggested in 1925 that they be called "cosmic rays" and that is what they are now known as. "Cosmic" also means vast and all-important, like the universe itself and a "cosmopolitan" is one who considers himself to be part of the whole world rather than part of but one small section of it. On the other hand, a small world, such as an anthill is a "microcosm," "micro" meaning "small."

There is an even better-known trace of "cosmos." Since cosmos means good arrangement, the powder, rouge, lipstick, mascara and other means of putting a face into better arrangement are "cosmetics." And, sure enough, to see some beauticians at work does indeed make it look as though they are using make up to form a Cosmos out of a Chaos.

In most systems of myths, the first beings to be formed out of the original chaos are not men, but gods. Gods are usually pictured as having the appearance of men, though sometimes they are partly or entirely animal in appearance. They differ from men in that they are much more powerful. They can control the forces of nature. They can direct the sun, or hurl lightning, or lash the sea with hurricanes, or make the plants grow, or let loose plague. Usually, they are pictured as immortal.

In the most familiar form of the Greek myths, the first beings to come out of chaos were *Gaia* and *Ouranos*. Now "gaia" is the Greek word for "earth," and "ouranos" is the Greek word for "sky," so this is like saying that out of the original Chaos, Earth and Sky were formed.

The Greeks pictured the earth as female (we ourselves speak of "mother Earth") and so Gaia was not only the physical earth itself, but also a female god (a "goddess") that symbolized the earth. She was the "goddess of the earth." In the same way, Ouranos was the "god of the sky."

Eventually, when the Latin-speaking Romans conquered Greece, they were fascinated by the Greek way of life and adopted as much of it as they could. They were very interested in the Greek gods and goddesses, for instance. However, in writing of these gods and goddesses, they spelled the names according to a system of their own. The Latin alphabet was different from that of the Greeks and to keep the correct pronunciation, they had to change the letter combinations.

For instance, there is no "k" in the Latin alphabet so

wherever the Greeks used a "k," as in "kosmos," the Romans used a "c" as in "cosmos." Where the Greeks used "ou" and "ai," the Romans usually substituted "u" and "ae." The Greeks often ended names with "os," but the Romans almost always changed that to "us."

Thus the Roman spelling of the name of the Greek goddess of the earth is *Gaea*, and for the Greek god of the sky, *Uranus*.

Our modern English names generally follow the Roman spelling rather than the Greek, because our alphabet is almost the same as the Latin alphabet. Often, however, we simplify the names by dropping the final "us," or changing a final "ius" to a final "y." In this book, I will use the English versions of the Latin spellings.

However, our pronunciation of letter combinations is not the same as the Roman pronunciation. For instance, "Gaia" in Greek and "Gaea" in Latin are both pronounced "Gay'yuh." We, however, pronounce it "Jee'uh." Again the Greek "Ouranos" and the Latin "Uranus" are both pronounced "Oo'-ruh-nus" but we pronounce it "You'ruh-nus." In this book, I will give the English pronunciation of the names when that seems necessary, but we must remember that this is not always the way the ancients pronounced the word.

The Romans further identified their own gods and goddesses with those of the Greeks. That is, they would suppose one of their gods or goddesses was the same as a particular Greek god or goddess. Then they would substitute their own name for the Greek one. Since many modern European languages developed out of Latin, the Latin names ended up more familiar to us than the Greek names.

For instance, the Roman goddess of the earth had two names, *Terra* and *Tellus*. Both of these were identified with Gaea, and both are more often used in English than Gaea is. Thus, in science-fiction stories, a human being may be called an "Earthling," a "Terrestrial" or a "Tellurian," but never a "Gaean." Again, a being from another planet is almost always called an "extra-terrestrial," where "extra" is the Latin word for "outside."

Terra appears in more familiar words, too. A raised

bank of earth is a "terrace" and the shape of the landscape about us is the "terrain." The tract of land over which a nation exists is its "territory."

Tellus has not left as many traces, but one important one is to be found in chemistry. In 1798, a German chemist named Martin Heinrich Klaproth suggested a name for a new element that had been discovered fifteen years earlier. He had already named an element for the sky, and he felt he ought to give the earth similar credit. He chose Tellus to symbolize the earth and he named the element "tellurium."

However, Gaea is not entirely forgotten. There are a number of English words that have the prefix "geo-" to remind us of that ancient goddess.

The most familiar of these are "geography" ("description of the earth"), "geology" ("science of the earth"), and "geometry" ("measurement of the earth"). The first use of geometry was, in fact, the surveying or measuring of the earth, in order that the boundaries of farms might be determined.

Again, the Greek theory that the earth was at the center of the universe and that the sun, moon and planets revolve about it is called the "geocentric theory."

The study of the physical processes on and within the earth, such as its heat or magnetism or the movement of currents in the sea or winds in the air, is "geophysics." Thus, the "International Geophysical Year" which ran from July 1, 1957, to December 31, 1958, and during which the first man-made satellites were launched, contains a reference to Gaea.

Similar words are based on Uranus. "Uranography" is the description of the constellations of the sky and "uranology" is the science of the sky (for which the more common word, however, is "astronomy").

Uranus, however, gained a fame in modern science that none of the Earth goddesses could match. In 1781, a German-born English astronomer, William Herschel, discovered a new planet more distant than any that were known before. Until that date, all the planets that were known were bright objects in the sky that were easily seen and that had been recognized in prehistoric times. The new planet was a very faint object, however, barely visible to the naked eye.

Herschel wanted to call the new planet "Georgium Sidus" (which is Latin for "George's star") after George III, who was then King of England. Other astronomers suggested it be named "Herschel" after the discoverer.

Neither suggestion was adopted. All the other planets had been named after ancient gods and goddesses and the custom was kept. The new planet was named Uranus at the suggestion of a German astronomer named Johann Bode.

The discovery of the new planet created quite a sensation and Uranus thus gained a new fame that brought his name to the lips of many men who had never heard, or who had forgotten, the Greek myth. However, something happened a few years after the discovery of Uranus which, eventually, made the god's name even more sensational.

In 1789, Klaproth (the chemist I mentioned a bit earlier) discovered a new metal. Now it had been an old-fashioned habit of the chemists of the Middle Ages to name metals after the planets in the sky. Klaproth felt he ought to name his new metal after the new planet, so he called the metal "uranium" (and later named another element tellurium, to balance matters, as I said above).

Nowadays, as the result of the development of the atomic bomb, the word uranium is famous indeed. The oldest of the Greek gods still lives in a word connected with the newest and most dreadful of scientific weapons.

Uranus and Gaea were considered by the ancient Greeks as man and wife, giving birth to children. Picture the rain falling from the sky (Uranus) to the earth (Gaea) and bringing about the growth of plants, and you can see that the Greeks were symbolizing this when they talked of marriage and children.

Many of the children of this ancient couple were ferocious beings of tremendous size and power, called *Gigantes,* or, in English, "giants." These probably represented the destructive forces of nature.

From these giants, we get the word "gigantic" for anything of very large size. A person who grows to unusual heights because of hormone troubles is said, by doctors, to suffer from "gigantism." Circus giants are usually sufferers of this disease.

Many of the giants were monstrous as well as large. Some were pictured as having a hundred arms. Others possessed a single, staring eye in the middle of the forehead. These were called *Cyclops*, which in Greek means "round-eyed." They were supposed to work in forges in volcanoes, from whence mysterious rumblings could often be heard and from which molten rock and ashes occasionally shot out when, the Greeks supposed, the fires of the forge grew too high. The Cyclops might well symbolize volcanoes altogether, since the volcano has a crater at the top, like a single eye, staring at heaven.

The Cyclops were also supposed to manufacture the lightning bolts, so that they eventually came to symbolize that form of destructive power as well. In fact, the first three Cyclops born of Uranus and Gaea, were named *Brontes, Steropes, and Arges,* which are the Greek words for "thunder," "lightning," and "brightness." This is one way of saying that when rain descends from Uranus to Gaea, thunder and lightning are sometimes born of the process and a brightness results. Brontes is sometimes used as a term for a blacksmith.

The Cyclops were supposed to have built the walls of Mycenae and Tiryns, two cities that were the most powerful of all in the very early days of Greece. When Greece was at its height, however, those two cities were merely ruined villages and the Greeks then wondered how they came to have such huge walls made of tremendous rocks fitted together without mortar. They decided that only giant beings, like the Cyclops, could have piled those rocks.

As a result, even today, walls made of large rocks without mortar are called "cyclopean." In fact, the word is a less familiar synonym of "gigantic." Yet Cyclops is a name given to a tiny water flea not more than a twentieth of an inch long. The name isn't given it because of its size of course, but because it seems to have a single eye in the middle of its head. (Actually, though, the eye is double.)

2 THE TITANS

THE MOST IMPORTANT of the gigantic offspring of Uranus and Gaea were a group of creatures, both male and female, who were called *Titans* and *Titanesses*. Since the Greeks presented these usually (but not always) as tremendous giants, the word "titan" has become synonymous with "giant." Something which is described as "gigantic" may also be described as "titanic."

In 1911, a giant ship, the largest in existence at that time, was launched. To express its size, it was named the *Titanic*. It was thought to be so large and so advanced as to be unsinkable. In fact, so certain were the builders and owners of its unsinkability that they didn't bother very much with such things as lifeboats, life preservers, emergency drills and so on.

On April 14, 1912, on its very first voyage, it struck an iceberg. The supposedly unsinkable ship sank in less than three hours. Of the 2206 passengers, over 1500 drowned. It was the greatest ship disaster in all history.

Perhaps if the owners had known mythology and been

more superstitious they might have avoided such a boastful name. That was the kind of pride which the Greeks believed was sure to be followed by destruction, as I shall explain later in the book. Besides, the Titans themselves underwent complete destruction in the myths, so to use their name may have been a bad omen, superstitious people might think.

Turning to chemistry again, Klaproth, who had introduced the names of Uranus and of Tellus (the Roman Gaea) into the list of elements, did the same for their sons, the Titans. In 1791, a new metal had been discovered by an English clergyman named William Gregor. Klaproth's suggestion that it be named "titanium" was accepted.

As a matter of fact, that name turns out, quite by coincidence, to be a good one. When titanium is impure it is rather brittle and useless. Recently, however, chemists have succeeded in preparing titanium in quite pure form, and it then turns out to be the strongest metal known. The name titanium fits its titanic strength.

Some prehistoric animals of great size are also named for these giants of mythology. There is a type of dinosaur called "titanosaurus" ("titanic lizard") and, for that matter, one called "gigantosaurus" ("giant lizard") and another called "brontosaurus" ("thunder lizard") which recalls Brontes, one of the Cyclops I mentioned earlier. There is also an ancient species of giant rhinoceros called "titanotherium" ("titanic beast").

The most powerful of the Titans was *Cronus*. He led a revolt of the Titans against their father, Uranus. Gaea had grown tired of giving birth to giants and monsters. Consequently, she armed Cronus with a scythe and with this he attacked Uranus and drove him away.

In this manner, the Greeks may have symbolized their belief that originally earth and sky were close together. Cronus and his brother Titans symbolized the sun, moon and planets which drove earth and sky apart and took over the vast space between. In this way, the universe was put into its final shape.

The word Cronus is not Greek in its origin and is

probably a hangover from those who inhabited Greece before the Greeks themselves arrived. It was easy to suppose that the unfamiliar word, Cronus, was actually the familiar Greek word "Chronos," meaning "time."

For that reason, Cronus was frequently considered to be the "god of time." Even today, "Father Time" is usually pictured as an old man carrying a scythe, the weapon with which Cronus defeated Uranus. That is the most familiar way in which Cronus lingers on into modern times and it is a wrong one. (An old woman is sometimes called a "crone" but this has no connection with Cronus. It comes from an old Danish word and the similarity is a coincidence.)

To the people who preceded the Greeks, Cronus was probably a god of agriculture. The scythe with which he was supposed to have attacked his father, Uranus, was originally a tool for harvesting grain, nothing more deadly than that.

The Romans had a god of agriculture called *Saturn*, and they identified him with Cronus. The Romans honored Saturn during a week-long celebration from the 19th to the 26th of December. This celebration was called the "Saturnalia." There was great jollity, much feasting, and an exchange of presents. Some of the atmosphere lingers on into our modern celebration of Christmas at the same time of year.

However, so much wildness and drunkenness developed during the celebration that nowadays the word "saturnalia" means a wild, drunken party.

The Greeks associated Cronus with the sixth planet (counting our earth as one of the planets, the third). This may be because, of the planets known to the Greeks, the sixth planet was farthest from the earth and therefore the nearest to the outer limits of the sky. Could it be that it seemed to be leading the attack against the god of the sky (Uranus) and was therefore rightly named Cronus?

Another possibility is this. The sixth planet is also the farthest planet from the sun of all the planets known to the Greeks. The sun's gravitation is weak at that distance and the sixth planet moves more slowly than any other planet the Greeks knew. It moves so slowly that it takes

29½ years to make a complete circuit of the sky against the background of the stars. With such a slow and majestic movement, it might have seemed to the Greeks that it ought to be symbolized by an old, old god. Cronus seemed the natural choice.

The Romans naturally called the planet "Saturn" and that is the name that has come down to us.

Saturn has a thin set of rings encircling it about its equator. The ancients didn't know this, of course, since the rings are invisible without a telescope. They were discovered in 1655, and in that same year the first of Saturn's nine satellites was discovered. This satellite was number six (counting outward from Saturn) and was named "Titan." This is a poor name, really, because it isn't the name of a god, but of a whole group of gods.

Most of the remaining satellites of Saturn were named after individual Titans and Titanesses, for it seemed fitting to associate them with Saturn in the heavens. Thus, satellites seven and eight were named *Hyperion* (high-pee'ree-on) and *Iapetus* (eye-ap'i-tus) after Titans. Satellites three, four, five and nine were named *Tethys* (tee'this), *Dione* (die-oh'nee), *Rhea* (ree'uh), and *Phoebe* (fee'bee) after Titanesses. In 1905, a satellite was reported as discovered and was named *Themis* (thee'mis), after a Titaness who was later considered the goddess of justice. The discovery proved to be a mistake and, as far as we know, no such satellite exists.

Of all the Titanesses memorialized among Saturn's satellites, Rhea was the most important. She was the wife of Cronus and since she was also associated with agriculture originally, she is another version of the earth goddess. She was the mother, as I shall explain later, of the chief gods and goddesses actually worshiped by the Greeks, so she was called "The Mother of the Gods" and was held in high honor. (For some reason, her name has been given to a group of ostrichlike birds, the "rheas," who are to be found in South America.)

About 200 B.C. the Romans took over a goddess named *Cybele* (si'bi-lee) who was originally worshiped in Asia Minor as a goddess of agriculture. The Romans identified her with Rhea and worshiped her as "Magna Mater"

("Great Mother") or "Alma Mater" ("Fostering Mother"). That phrase "alma mater" is now applied to a man's college, which has been a fostering mother, one that feeds and protects, to his mind.

Not all the Titans and Titanesses are memorialized among the satellites of Saturn. Tethys, the Titaness, is there, to be sure, but her husband, *Oceanus* (Oh-see'uh-nus), is not.

Oceanus was the oldest of the Titans and symbolized the water that encircled the land of the world. The Greeks weren't sure that water encircled all the land, of course. They were only familiar with the Mediterranean Sea and the land about it. That means southern Europe, northern Africa and western Asia.

In three of the four directions, they knew only of continuous land (which is why Europe, Asia and Africa, and any large stretch of land is called a "continent"). However, the Mediterranean Sea stretched off westward until it came to what we call today the Strait of Gibraltar. There, Europe and Africa almost meet, but not quite. And beyond it is a vast stretch of open water.

This water seemed to run far north and south and to the Greeks it seemed to be a neat and satisfactory arrangement to have it in the form of a tremendous circular river occupying the rim of a pie-plate world.

However, since the only part of this world-river they actually knew about lay in the far west, they imagined Oceanus and Tethys to live out there. In fact, the ancient Greeks put most of their wonders in the far west.

Of course as men grew to know the world better, it was found that the world-river was not a river at all, but a vast stretch of open salt water like the Mediterranean but much larger. The name of the Titan lingers on, however, for of course we call such a large stretch of water an "ocean."

The Greeks turned out to be right in one respect about the world-river. Water does indeed extend all around Europe, Asia and Africa, but there are other large tracts of land besides. There is North and South America, Antarctica, Australia, and a host of smaller islands. These break up the continuous stretch of salt water, so that now we speak of five different oceans.

Because New Guinea and thousands of smaller islands are surrounded by the largest of the oceans, the Pacific Ocean, they are lumped together under the name of "Oceania." Thus, land the Greeks never saw is named after the Titan of their imagination.

As for Tethys, the wife of Oceanus, she has received her memorial (aside from being a satellite of Saturn) in a less common way. Scientists, tracing the past history of the earth, have learned that the pattern of land and sea was not always the same. Some hundreds of millions of years ago, there was a large stretch of water, running from the Atlantic to the Pacific Ocean across Asia. The Mediterranean Sea is a modern remnant of that ancient stretch of water. The Austrian geologist Eduard Suess named it the "Tethys Sea."

Perhaps the best known of all the Titans is *Atlas*. He may or may not have been a second-generation Titan. That is, some of the ancient Greek writers describe him as a son of Uranus and a brother of Cronus, Oceanus, Iapetus and the other Titans. Others describe him as the son of Iapetus and the grandson of Uranus, so that he would be the nephew of Cronus and Oceanus.

This is not very important except that it shows there is nothing certain in mythology. Each Greek writer felt free to tell the myths in his own way and the information you get depends on the one read.

In any case, Atlas joined the other Titans in a war against younger and more powerful gods. He may even have been the Titan general. He and the other Titans were defeated and, as punishment, Atlas was condemned to support the heavens on his shoulders. (In fact, the name "Atlas" comes from a Greek word meaning "to support.")

The Greeks pictured Atlas as standing in the far west near the straits of Gibraltar, their usual misty region of wonders. When the western region was better explored, they naturally found no Atlas there, but they did find a region of mountains, so they decided that at some time in the past, Atlas had been turned to stone. The range of mountains in Morocco and Algeria are still called the "Atlas Mountains."

Atlas was supposed to have been the father of various groups of young goddesses called the *Atlantides* (At-lan'ti-deez). They were also called the *Hesperides* (Hes-per'i-deez) from a Greek word meaning "west" because, like their father, they were pictured as dwelling in the far west.

To the ancient Greeks, by the way, any minor goddess pictured as a young girl was a *nymph,* which was the Greek word for "young girl." In zoology, the young forms of certain insects are called "nymphs," for this reason.

The Greeks pictured the nymphs as symbolizing the various objects of nature. There were nymphs living in trees, in rocks and mountains, in lakes and rivers. They were what we might call the "spirit" of a particular tree or a particular brook.

The Atlantides were nymphs associated with the sea. Other such nymphs were the *Oceanids*, the daughters of Oceanus, of course, and the *Nereids,* the daughters of an old god of the sea named Nereus.

The Atlantides were associated with the far western waters of Oceanus, so that those waters were called "Atlantic" as well as "Ocean" and today we call it "Atlantic Ocean." Thus both Atlas and Oceanus leave their traces on the name of the second largest ocean, to say nothing of such cities as Atlanta, Georgia, and Atlantic City and Ocean City in New Jersey.

In 355 B.C., when the Greek philosopher Plato made up a story about a great land in the western Ocean which sank beneath the waters after an earthquake, he called it "Atlantis." It was pure fiction, of course, but there have been people ever since who have insisted that Atlantis really existed.

As time went on, it became difficult to picture Atlas as holding up the sky. The Greeks learned more about astronomy and decided that the sky had to be at least millions of miles from the earth. Besides, they decided, the sky has no tendency to fall and need not be held up.

So the notion arose of Atlas supporting the earth rather than the sky. In fact, when Atlas is pictured these days it is as a gigantic, weary figure with the great globe of the earth weighing down on one shoulder while he steadies it with one tremendous arm.

There is a bone in the human body which seems to do the job of Atlas. The globe of the head rests on the spine, which is made up of a series of bones running down the length of the back. The topmost one of these bones, which supports the head, is naturally called the "atlas."

Now when the early geographers began to make books of maps of various regions of the earth, they used to put on the cover a picture of Atlas holding up the earth. In the 1500's, the Flemish geographer Gerhardus Mercator drew up the first modern maps, and he called his book of such maps an "atlas" from the picture on the cover.

Ever since, a book of maps—and, indeed, any book of drawings or pictures illustrating some subject, such as the anatomy of a human being—is called an atlas.

In zoology, Atlas, like Titan, can be used to indicate tremendous size. An ancient dinosaur that is supposed to have been the largest of all, stretching a hundred feet from the tip of its head to the end of its long tail, is called "Atlantosaurus" (the "Atlas-like lizard"). Similarly, the "Atlas beetle" is a very large beetle and the "Atlas moth" a very large moth.

And very modern examples are two powerful ballistic missiles being built by the United States, the "Atlas" and the "Titan." An even more powerful missile is the "Saturn."

The Titan Hyperion, who is included as one of the satellites of Saturn, was originally considered the god of the sun. However, as time went on, this became the function of Hyperion's son, *Helios* (Hee′-lee-os).

Perhaps the most important trace of Helios in modern English is the result of an eclipse of the sun that took place in India in 1868. The light of the sun's glowing atmosphere was allowed to pass through an instrument called a spectroscope. In doing so, the light was split up into a series of bright lines of different colors. Each line was the mark of a particular element in the sun's atmosphere and could be duplicated in the light of elements known on earth when these were heated to a white-hot glow. There was but one exception. One line in the sun's light was not like the line produced by any known element on the earth.

The British astronomer Norman Lockyer decided it must be produced by an element that occurred only in the sun. He named that element "helium."

Twenty-seven years later, that element was discovered on the earth, too, but by then the name was firmly stuck. The element is still called helium, the "element of the sun."

The prefix "helio-" is used in a number of words having to do with the sun. For instance, the modern picture of the Solar system is that of a series of planets circling the sun as a center and this is the "heliocentric theory."

A more common example involves a flower which turns constantly toward the sun. The most common flower of this sort is called, in straightforward English, the "sunflower." A less common example is the "heliotrope," which, in Greek, means "turn toward the sun."

Hyperion, the father of Helios, was also pictured as having two daughters, *Selene* (se-lee′nee) and *Eos* (ee′os). The first was goddess of the moon, the second, goddess of the dawn. Thus, the three children of Hyperion symbolized the three important sources of light on the earth; the sun, the moon, and the light of dawn that spreads over the earth before the sun rises. (Of course, the light of dawn is caused by the sun shining on the upper atmosphere before its light reaches the ground itself, but the mythmakers either didn't know this or didn't care.)

Like Helios, Selene leaves traces in the table of chemical elements. In 1818, a Swedish chemist, Jöns Jacob Berzelius, discovered an element very like tellurium; a kind of twin sister, so to speak. Since tellurium had been named after a goddess of the earth (as I explained earlier in the book), Berzelius decided to balance matters by naming the new element after a goddess of the moon. He chose Selene and named the new element "selenium."

Eos, the third source of light, does not enter the list of elements, but she is not forgotten. Eos symbolized not only the dawn to the Greeks, but also the direction in which it appeared. The English word for that direction is "east" which, as you see, is similar.

The prefix "eo-" is used in words meaning anything which occurs at the very beginning, the dawn, of something. For instance, after the dinosaurs died out, a period in earth's history began in which the birds and mammals were most important. This is the "Cenozoic" period from Greek words meaning "new animals."

Well, the first part of the Cenozoic period is called the "Eocene" ("dawn of the new").

Then, again, scientists have studied the bones of very ancient horselike animals. The oldest ancestor of the modern horse which they could find was an animal no larger than a fox, with four toes on each foot. This is called "Eohippus" ("dawn horse").

Finally, primitive tools are found in the ground which were left behind by ancient men hundreds of thousands of years ago. The oldest of all are so primitive, scientists can't be quite sure whether they were formed by men or whether they just took on crude tool-like shapes by the accidental action of wind and water. Those most primitive tools are called "eoliths" ("dawn stones").

The Romans had their own gods and goddesses of these various forms of light. They identified their god *Sol* with Helios, their goddess *Luna* with Selene, and their goddess *Aurora* (Aw-ro'ruh) with Eos. In each case, it is the Roman name that is better known in English.

The word "solar" is a common adjective in English to describe anything pertaining to the sun, and "lunar" serves the same purpose in connection with the moon.

For instance, the sun, and the planets circling it, are called the "solar system." The period of time in which the earth circles the sun just once is the "solar year." On the other hand, the period of time in which the moon circles the earth just once is a "lunar month." Twelve lunar months is a "lunar year," which is eleven days shorter than a solar year.

There are other traces too. A room open to the sun for sun-bathing purposes is a "solarium." A small sunshade is a "parasol," a word which comes from Italian words meaning "to guard against the sun." As for the moon, its most dramatic shape is, of course, the crescent, and to say something is "lunate" is to say it is crescent-shaped.

The Roman goddess Aurora leaves her name on a very beautiful phenomenon indeed. Tiny particles called electrons are fired out from the sun and collect in the space around the earth because they are trapped there by the earth's magnetism. There is always a slow leakage of these electrons down into the earth's atmosphere in the far north and far south. There, the earth's magnetism is strongest.

When the electrons strike the atoms of the upper atmosphere, they cause them to glow in faint colors. As seen from the surface of the earth, colored sheets and streamers appear in the sky. This is very common in the polar regions, but is only occasionally seen as far south as London or New York.

When it is, there is always amazement that light like the light of dawn should appear in the north rather than in the east. We call this phenomenon the "Northern Lights" in plain English. The French astronomer, Pierre Gassendi, called it the "Aurora Borealis" ("northern dawn") in 1621. Then, in 1773, the English explorer, James Cook, sailed far enough south to see the "Southern Lights" and these he called "Aurora Australis" ("southern dawn").

There were daughters of Uranus and Gaea who were neither giants nor Titans. Some of them, however, represented terrors that were more frightful than mere monstrous size and shape could be. For instance, there were the three *Erinnyes* (Uh-rin'i-eez). These sisters punished those who were guilty of particularly horrible crimes. They pursued them, gave them no rest and drove them mad. Probably they symbolized conscience and remorse, those feelings inside a man which can indeed bring him lifelong misery over a wrong he regrets having committed.

The Greeks often called these sisters the *Eumenides* (Yoo-men'i-deez), meaning the "kindly ones," in order to keep them kindly by telling them that was what they were. (This habit of calling something unpleasant by a pleasant name in order to avoid unpleasantness is called "euphemism" from Greek words meaning "To speak well.")

The Romans called these avenging women *Furia* ("Furies" in English) and we inherit the word "fury" as a result. Originally, this meant a kind of raging madness of the sort brought on by the Furies, one in which a person was not responsible for his deeds. A woman, in particular, behaving in this fashion, is called a Fury. With time, the word weakened, and now to be "furious" means only to be very angry.

Another set of three ancient sisters are the *Moirae*. These may be the daughters, or the nieces of Uranus. They controlled the course of the universe. The Greeks felt that the entire course was laid out at the beginning and could not be altered. Even the gods were helpless to interfere.

The three Moirae were named *Clotho* (kloh'thoh), *Lachesis* (lak'is-is), and *Atropos* (at'ro-pos).

Clotho is pictured as spinning all the threads that represent life for all the individuals alive. In fact the name means "the spinner" in Greek. In ordinary life, threads that are spun are usually woven into "cloth" out of which, most often, "clothes" are made. These English words come from the Anglo-Saxon, but they must be related to Clotho.

The word "lachesis" means "lot" in Greek. They imagined each child as drawing some lot when he was born which decided what his life would be like. Lachesis controls the nature of this lot by guiding and measuring the length of thread spun by Clotho.

Of course, Lachesis doesn't work by chance. Some Greeks thought that a person's lot was what he deserved, or what he "merited" and the word "merit" is related to "Moirae." It is possible to merit either good or evil but naturally everyone wants to merit good and the word has been slanted in that direction. To say someone or something "has merit" implies that it is good or worthwhile.

Finally, at the point indicated by Lachesis, Atropos, who is usually pictured with a pair of shears, cuts the cord. That meant death. "Atropos" in Greek means "not turning." Atropos was not to be turned away from her purpose by anyone or anything. There was no way of stopping her.

Atropos leaves a trace of herself in modern chemistry.

There is a plant called "belladonna" (Italian for "beautiful lady") from which a juice can be obtained for use as eyedrops. Such eyedrops cause the pupils of the eye to enlarge. Women using these drops felt that this gave their eyes a beautiful dark appearance, which is why the plant received its name.

The belladonna juice, however, is very poisonous, if swallowed. When the Swedish botanist, Carolus Linnaeus, was classifying plants in the late 1700's, he gave the belladonna group the general name "Atropa." The belladonna plant, in other words, could cut the thread of life as surely as Atropos ever could. Then, in 1831, the poisonous chemical in belladonna juice was located and named "atropine."

The Romans also visualized three sisters determining the lot of men. They called them the *Parcae* (par'see) from a Latin word meaning "to bring forth" because the actions of these sisters brought forth the future. The Romans (and the Greeks, too) believed that they didn't always have to wait till the end to see what future would bring forth. They felt the future could be revealed in advance by the gods. Systems for revealing the future were called "oracles," from a Latin word meaning "to speak," because a common way of receiving an oracle was to have a priestess go into a trance and speak what were supposedly the words of the god.

The priestesses were usually careful to pronounce oracles that didn't predict the future too clearly but could be interpreted in at least two different ways. Thus, they played it safe. For that reason, an "oracular" statement is one which does not have a straightforward meaning but can be taken either way. The most famous oracle of all was at a Greek town named Delphi, so such a confusing statement can also be said to be "delphic."

Another word for oracle was "fatum," from another Latin word meaning "to speak." Since oracles dealt with the future, which was, after all, decided by the three Parcae (or Moirae), the Romans called the three sisters "Fata" also.

In English, we therefore speak of the "Three Fates"

and also of "fate" as meaning a future which cannot be changed. A person who believes that nothing in the future can be changed, that all is decided upon in advance, is a "fatalist."

The third of the Parcae, by the way, whom the Romans identified with Atropos is *Morta,* from a Latin word meaning "death." She is what we would call the "Angel of Death."

We use the word often enough. Man is "mortal" because he is fated to die; the gods are "immortal" ("not dying"). A wound is "mortal" if it brings death and a "mortician" is an undertaker.

The Greeks recognized a softer side to death. After a long and weary life, death might even come as a rest. For that reason, they considered *Thanatos,* the god of death, to be a brother of Hypnos, the god of sleep.

Thanatos has not left any well-known traces, but he enters the history of American literature. The first great American poem was written in 1817 by William Cullen Bryant who was then twenty-three years old. Despite his age, it dwelt on the theme of death and he called it "Thanatopsis," which in Greek means "the sight of death."

Hypnos probably strikes a familiar note. An artificial sleep brought on by drugs or by suggestion is "hypnosis," and a sleeping pill is a "hypnotic."

The Roman god of sleep is *Somnus.* When we are sleepy, we are "somnolent." Sleepwalking is "somnambulism" which in Latin means exactly that, "sleepwalking."

The son of Somnus is *Morpheus* (mor'fyoos), the god of dreams. (After all, sleep does give birth to dreams.) "Morpheus" goes back through Latin to the Greek word for "form" or "shape" because dreams are forms and shapes brought before the mind's eye.

"Morphology" is that branch of biology that deals with the form and structure of living things. On the other hand, add the prefix "a-" (which is a Greek method for turning a word into its opposite) and you have the word "amorphous" meaning "shapeless."

The god of dreams leaves an interesting trace in chemistry. A German chemist, F. W. Sertürner, in 1803, isolated the first pure chemical to be obtained from a natural plant medicine. It was a powerful hypnotic. To people in agonizing pain, it brought relief and sleep. It was like Morpheus himself coming to enfold them—so the chemical was named "morphine."

But although the Greeks felt so strongly that Fate ruled life and could not be altered, they also recognized the existence of chance. The goddess of chance, described as a daughter of Oceanus, was named *Tyche* (tie'kuh). This is not nearly as familiar to us as the Roman equivalent, *Fortuna* (for-tyoo'nuh).

Thus, we speak of a person's "fortune" as signifying the fate that awaits him through the workings of chance and a person who pretends to predict the future is a "fortune-teller." Naturally, everyone hopes his future will be a happy one and the young man who goes out into the world to "seek his fortune" hopes it will turn out to involve much money. Consequently a large sum of money is described as a "fortune"; a happy or lucky person is said to be "fortunate," while a sad or unlucky one is "unfortunate."

Fortuna is the name of one of the planetoids, by the way; that of the nineteenth to be discovered.

3 THE OLYMPIANS

THE RULE of the Titans under Cronus did not endure. After Uranus had been defeated and driven off by Cronus, the old god of the sky predicted that Cronus would be treated in the same way by one of his own sons. Therefore, every time Rhea bore a child, Cronus would swallow it.

This picture of Cronus swallowing his children had an odd follow-up in the history of astronomy. The Italian scientist Galileo Galilei was the first to use a telescope to view the heavens. When he turned it on distant Saturn (the Roman name for Cronus, remember) he just barely made out the rings.

Unfortunately, his telescope was too weak to let him make them out clearly. He could only see what looked like two bulges, one on each side of Saturn. Galileo said it was as though old Saturn needed two young sons, one on each side, to help his faltering steps through space.

However, the rings are seen at different angles, depending on the positions of Saturn and the earth in their journeys about the sun. Occasionally, we see the rings edge-on and they are so thin that at such a time they seem to disappear. When Galileo came to look at Saturn again, that happened to be the situation and he found the two bulges gone. Puzzled and disappointed he exclaimed, "What! Does Saturn still swallow his children?" He did not look at Saturn again and it was left to Huyghens to see the rings as they actually were about half a century later.

Cronus did not, however, save himself by swallowing his children. Rhea, annoyed by this habit of her husband's, dressed a stone in baby clothes and fed it to him in place of her sixth and last child. This last child was *Zeus* (Zoos).

Zeus was secretly raised on the island of Crete, south of Greece. There he was fed on milk supplied by a goat named *Amaltheia* (am'al-thee'uh). When he had grown to manhood, his mother Rhea helped him trick Cronus into taking a drink that caused the Titan to throw up Zeus's five brothers and sisters. Since they were immortal gods, they were all alive and well.

Zeus, his brothers and sisters and their descendants were called the "Olympians" because the Greeks pictured them as dwelling on Mount Olympus. This mountain, the highest mountain in Greece, nearly ten thousand feet high, stands near the northern boundary of the country. (Of course, later on, the Greeks came to realize that there weren't really any signs of gods on Mount Olympus and they decided that the real Olympus was high in heaven.)

In the region of Elis, in southwestern Greece, there were special games every four years in honor of Zeus. The valley in which they were celebrated was called "Olympia" in honor of Mount Olympus, and in later years Phidias, Greece's greatest sculptor, carved a statue of "Olympian Zeus" for the site of the games. This statue was considered one of the seven wonders of the ancient world.

The first of these "Olympian games" of which there is a record were conducted in 776 B.C. These games were the great event of the Greek world. Winners at the competitions were heaped with honors and the Greeks even counted the years by these games. Every four years was an "Olympiad" and each Olympiad was numbered. With the coming of Christianity, the games were frowned upon as a pagan festival. The Roman Emperor Theodosius put an end to them in A.D. 394 after nearly 300 Olympiads.

In 1896, they were revived and the first of the modern version of the games, called the "Olympic games" rather than the Olympian games, was conducted in Greece. Since then, they have been held in various countries, including, several times, in the United States. Except for interruptions during World War I and World War II, they have been continued every four years, as in ancient times. And so we still honor Olympian Zeus, at least in the name we give these games.

To return to the myths—The Olympians, having been rescued from Cronus, accepted the leadership of Zeus, and rebelled against the Titans. The Titans were the stronger as far as brute force was concerned. Zeus, however, took as allies the Cyclops whom, earlier, the Titans had imprisoned. The Cyclops forged lightning bolts for Zeus and by use of the lightning, Zeus defeated the Titans. He imprisoned some of them underground and condemned Atlas, their leader, to hold up the heavens. Some Titans, such as Oceanus, who had remained neutral or even joined the Olympians, were left in peace.

This battle between the Titans and the Olympians may have been a symbolic description of the invasion of the land now called Greece by the first Greeks. These brought their gods with them, including Zeus, to displace or absorb the gods of the pre-Greek inhabitants.

The conquered population, who found themselves under the rule of the Greek strangers, gradually adopted the Greek language and Greek ways. However, they must have remembered their old life with some sorrow, for the exaggerated legend grew up that there had been a "Golden Age" under the rule of Cronus. Then everyone had been happy, eating nuts and fruits and drinking milk. There had been no misery or sickness, and death came easily, like his brother, sleep. We still speak of any time in a nation's history when it was particularly powerful, or particularly prosperous, as a "golden age" or a "Saturnian age."

The two brothers of Zeus were *Poseidon* (poh-sigh'-don) and *Hades* (hay'deez). After the victory over the Titans, it was agreed that Zeus was to remain the ruler of the Olympians, but the brothers cast lots to see what parts of the universe would be their special care. Zeus received the air, Poseidon the sea and Hades the underworld.

As Hades received the underworld, he was considered the god of the dead, for the underworld has always been associated with death. This is perhaps because of the habit of burying the dead underground. (The Greeks themselves in later times burned their dead, but in earlier times, when the myths were first made up, they buried their dead.) As a result, the place where the shades of the dead dwelt was called "Hades" after the god. The word "hades" comes from Greek words meaning "invisible" since the underground world cannot be seen.

Hades was thus not really an Olympian, for he did not live in Olympus. Rather he became one of the "chthonian gods" (tho'nee-an); that is, a "god of the underworld."

The Greeks had other chthonian gods and they were usually pictured as frightening and monstrous. They were thought of as having originated from Chaos by a line of birth that did not involve Uranus and Gaea. Chaos gave rise to *Nox*, the goddess of the darkness of night, and *Erebus*, the god of the darkness of the underground.

We still are referring to the goddess of night when we refer to things of the night as "nocturnal." Similarly, a musical composition meant to be played in the evening is a "nocturne." As for Erebus, there is a volcano of that name in Antarctica. It is a good name, too, if you think of the long, frigid Antarctic night and the grim crater of the volcano leading down into the further darkness of the underworld.

Erebus and Night are considered to be the parents of the Moirae, or Fates. They are also the parents of *Tartarus*, who was probably the god of the underworld before the invasion of the Greeks brought in the Olympians. Hades displaced Tartarus as Zeus displaced Cronus.

Some of the Greek mythmakers, however, kept both Hades and Tartarus. Hades was considered a place where the dead were not particularly mistreated. Beneath it, lower still, however, was Tartarus, where particularly evil men and gods were sent for punishment. It is Tartarus that probably gave rise to many of the Christian notions of Hell.

Tartarus left its trace in a tragic episode in history. In the 1200's, the Mongol tribes under Genghis Khan spread out of their central Asian homeland. They invaded China, Persia, Russia and Poland, killing and destroying. It was probably the most disastrous barbarian invasion in history.

The Mongols called themselves "Tatars." So dreadful was their invasion, though, that they seemed to convert the earth into Tartarus, and it was a natural mistake to call them "Tartars" instead.

As for Hades, the Greek mythmakers had much to say of it. For instance, Hades was described as being bounded by the river *Styx*. Anything pertaining to the Styx, and therefore to the underworld, is said to be "Stygian." This word is particularly used in the phrase "Stygian darkness" meaning a great darkness, the darkness of the underworld. For some reason the Styx was considered to be particularly holy in oath-making. An oath by the river Styx dare not be broken.

To enter Hades, one had to be ferried across the Styx by a grim old ferryman named *Charon* (kay'-ron), another son of Erebus and Nox. This name can be humorously applied to any ferryman.

On the other side of the Styx, the entrance to Hades itself is guarded by a three-headed monstrous dog, named *Cerberus* (sur'buh-rus). Again the name can be applied jokingly to any guardian. Cerberus allowed no one to pass who did not first throw him a ransom in the form of a piece of bread. For that reason, the phrase "to throw a sop to Cerberus" means to pay a bribe to some official in order to get something done.

Once within Hades, the spirits of the dead drink from a river named *Lethe* (lee'thee), a Greek word meaning "forgetfulness." In drinking, they forget about their former life and become listless, gibbering ghosts. We still speak of anything which causes forgetfulness as "Lethean." You are liable to be forgetful if you are sleepy or sluggish, and you are then said to be "lethargic." And since complete forgetfulness comes only with death, we speak of anything deadly as "lethal."

The spirits of the dead need not undergo only gloom and horror. Worthy spirits might go to a special section of Hades where all was blissful and happy. That section was supposed to be ruled over by Cronus rather than Hades, an echo of the legend of the Golden Age. This happy place was called *Elysium* (ee-li'zhee-um) or the *"Elysian Fields."* We still speak of Elysium as a place or time of great happiness and even use it as another word for "heaven." The French words for Elysian Fields are "Champs Elysées" and that is the name given to a beautiful boulevard in Paris.

Some mythmakers felt that the Elysian Fields couldn't be in Hades, and placed them in the far west along with other marvels. They were then called "Islands of the Blessed" or the "Fortunate Isles."

Of course, the underground isn't only an abode of the dead. It is also the source of metals, especially gold and silver. The god of wealth is *Plutus,* from which we get our word "plutocracy" to mean a government run by the wealthy.

As a master of the underground regions from which wealth came, the god Hades was also given a form of that name, and was called *Pluto*.

The Romans identified two of these brothers with gods of their own. They had a god of the sky called *Jupiter,* whom they identified with Zeus; and a god of springs and rivers named *Neptune*, whom they identified with Poseidon.

Both ended among the planets. The Greeks named the fifth planet after Zeus. This was a logical choice because the fifth planet was the brightest except for the evening and morning star. The evening star, however, only appeared for a few hours after sunset and the morning star only for a few hours before dawn, while the fifth planet often shines the whole night through.

The Romans, of course, used their own version of the name and it is as "Jupiter" that the planet is known to us.

The Romans had a second name for Jupiter, and that was *Jove*. It is not used much by itself except in the old-fashioned exclamation, "by Jove." However, when an adjective is needed, Jove rather than Jupiter is used. For instance, one never says the "Jupiterian satellites" but always the "Jovian satellites."

Neptune had to wait until modern times for a similar planetary honor. In the early 1800's, astronomers carefully observed the planet Uranus in order to determine its exact orbit around the sun. They found, to their surprise, that its actual movement lagged a bit behind what their calculations were predicting. Some believed there might be another planet beyond Uranus whose gravitational pull was slowing it slightly.

An English astronomer, John Couch Adams, and a French astronomer, Urbain J. J. Leverrier, unknown to each other, both calculated where such a planet must be to account for the effect on Uranus. They both came out with the same answer. Leverrier was the first to announce his results and in 1846 an astronomer in Berlin looked at the spot indicated by Leverrier and, behold, there was the eighth planet.

It was named "Neptune," not for any particular reason, but because Neptune was one important god who lacked a planet.

Even allowing for Neptune, the motion of Uranus still lagged a tiny bit. The American astronomer Percival Lowell, in the first years of the twentieth century, therefore searched for another still more distant planet. He failed, but his successors found the ninth planet in 1931.

The ninth planet moves farthest from the light of the sun and farthest into the darkness of the space between the stars, so it was named "Pluto." The first two letters of the name happened to be the initials of Percival Lowell.

Pluto is the only important planet to have a Greek name, rather than a Roman one. The Romans had a god of the underworld named *Dis* and sometimes said "Dis pater" ("Father Dis") when they meant Hades, but for some reason this did not make the impression on the Western World that the other Latin names of gods did.

The discovery of Neptune and Pluto had an echo in

chemistry during World War II. Uranium was the most complicated element known in 1940. All the elements were listed in a chart called a "periodic table" in the order of increasing complexity. The elements went from number 1 to number 92 and uranium was number 92.

In 1940, however, chemists at the University of California learned how to manufacture small quantities of new elements which fitted into the period table in places 93 and 94. These new elements were beyond uranium in the table and were therefore named for the planets beyond Uranus. Consequently, element number 93 is known as "neptunium" and element number 94 as "plutonium."

The planet Jupiter, as befits one named after the ruler of the gods, has the largest family of satellites in the Solar system. It has twelve. Four of these were discovered by Galileo in 1610. They were the first objects in the solar system to be discovered by the telescope and all are large satellites. Two are larger than our moon and the other two are only slightly smaller. Each of the satellites was named after some person closely connected with Zeus in the myths.

For instance, Zeus was at one time in love with a river nymph named *Io* (eye′oh). However, Zeus was married to *Hera* (hee′ruh), one of the daughters of Cronus and Rhea, and Hera was a jealous woman. Zeus turned Io into a white cow in order to hide her, but Hera suspected the cow. She sent a giant named *Argus* to watch her.

Now Argus had a hundred eyes and some eyes were always open and watching. For that reason, any watchful, wakeful person is said to be "Argus-eyed." Zeus, however, had Argus charmed to sleep, all hundred eyes of him, and then killed. Hera set the eyes of Argus in the tail of the peacock, which was her special bird. As a result, a bird closely related to the peacock is called the "Argus pheasant."

But Hera's suspicions of Io were now confirmed, so she sent a stinging fly to drive her from place to place, never letting her rest. The myth-makers now had Io wander all over the known world. At one point, she crossed the straits separating Europe and Asia at the point where

Istanbul is located and the straits received the name "Bosporus" meaning "cow crossing." (Another English equivalent would be "ox ford," and a very famous town and University has that name though not through any connection with Io.) At another time she swam across the strip of the Mediterranean that separates Greece from southern Italy, and that was therefore named the "Ionian Sea." Finally, she was allowed to find peace in Egypt.

A similar story is told of the Nymph *Callisto* (Ka-lis'toe). Zeus turned her into a bear to hide her from Hera. Or, perhaps, Hera did it to punish the nymph.

A case where it was Zeus himself that was turned into an animal involves a girl (not a nymph, but a human being) named *Europa* (Yoo-ro'puh). She lived in Phoenicia on the Asiatic coast of the Mediterranean. Zeus changed himself into a white bull that swam out of the sea when she was with her maids at the seashore. The bull seemed so beautiful and tame that Europa climbed on its back. At that point the bull seized its opportunity, plunged into the sea and swam to the island of Crete. Europa was the first human being to arrive in that part of the world, according to the mythmakers, so the continent of which Greece is a part was named "Europe" in her honor.

It was a young man who was involved in still another case. This was *Ganymede* (Gan'i-meed), a handsome young man who was carried off to Olympus by Zeus in the form of an eagle. There Ganymede served as cupbearer, passing out the drinks at the banquets.

As a result of these stories, the four Jovian satellites discovered by Galileo were named "Io," "Europa," "Ganymede," and "Callisto" in order of their distance from the planet. The third satellite, Ganymede, is the largest in the solar system. It is 3200 miles in diameter and more massive even than Titan.

It was not until 1892 that a fifth Jovian satellite was discovered, by an American astronomer, Edward Emerson Barnard. It was a small satellite, only 100 miles in diameter, circling Jupiter at a distance less than that of even the nearest of the large satellites.

This is sometimes called "Barnard's satellite," after its

discoverer, and sometimes "Jupiter V" because it was the fifth Jovian satellite to be discovered. Its semi-official name, however, is "Amaltheia" after the goat that nursed the infant Zeus. It seems logical that the nurse of his childhood should be closer to him in the heavens than any of the companions of his adulthood.

In the 1900's seven more Jovian satellites were discovered. All of them are very small and quite distant from Jupiter. None have as yet received any names.

Passing on to the planet Neptune, it has two satellites and both are related to it in mythology.

Thus Poseidon has a son named *Triton,* who is half man and half fish (a common Greek way of picturing the gods and goddesses of the sea). After Poseidon had brought on a storm, it was Triton's job to come to the surface and blow a blast on a horn made out of a large sea shell. At the sound of Triton's horn, the waves were calmed.

Only a month after the planet Neptune was discovered, a British astronomer, William Lassell, discovered it had a large satellite, one that was nearly as large as Titan or Ganymede. It was eventually named "Triton."

(To come back to earth, there is a kind of large sea snail that is also called "Triton" because its shell is like that which Triton was supposed to have used.)

In 1950, the American astronomer G. P. Kuiper discovered a second satellite of Neptune's, one that was much smaller than Triton. He named it "Nereid" after the fifty sea nymphs that attended Poseidon on his travels through the sea.

Pluto has no known satellites. Uranus, on the other hand, has five. However, the Uranian satellites are the only ones in the solar system that do not get their names from Greek or Roman mythology, so there is no need to mention them further.

In addition to the planets, the heavens also contain thousands of stars. These are "fixed stars" since, unlike the planets, they do not change position with respect to one another. They form patterns that do not change, night after night and year after year.

Shepherds and farmers, in prehistoric days, studied these patterns because they served as a calendar. The sun moves against the background of the stars and different stars are visible at night at different times of the year.

The easiest way to handle the situation was to divide the stars into convenient groups which are nowadays called "constellations" (from Latin words meaning "with stars"). Then one could say that when one constellation rose in the east at sunset, it was harvest; the rising of another at sunset would indicate planting time and so on.

The most important constellations in this connection would be those through which the sun actually passed on its path across the sky. There are twelve of these. The reason for the twelve is that the phases of the moon were also used to keep time. The moon went through its phases twelve times while the sun traveled through the constellations once. In other words, there are twelve months to the year and the sun spent one month in each of twelve constellations.

The natural way of telling one constellation from another is to notice the pattern of stars in each one. It was inevitable that as time went on, people would begin to make complicated pictures out of these patterns. Eight stars arranged in a "V" might seem to resemble the head of a bull with its horns. Stars arranged in a "C" might suggest first a bow, and then an archer.

As a result, many of the constellations are now pictured as animals or people. In fact the circle of twelve constellations through which the sun passes in its travels contains so many imaginary animals that it is called the "zodiac" from Greek words meaning "circle of animals."

The Greeks inherited most of these constellation-pictures from the Babylonians. What they then did was either to change the pictures to fit their own myths, or else invent myths to explain the pictures.

For instance, there is a constellation in the zodiac that is now known by its Latin name of *Capricornus* (kap-ri kor'nus) from Latin words meaning "horned goat."

The Greeks stated that this goat was actually Amaltheia which was placed in the skies by Zeus out of gratitude for the nourishment she gave him as an infant. If this is so, then Amaltheia leaves her traces in geography as well.

On December 21, the sun is as far south as it ever gets. It is then shining directly down on a line that passes through northern Argentina, southern Africa and central Australia. That line is called the "Tropic of Capricorn" because at that time of year the sun, in its travels, is in the constellation of Capricornus.

The constellations of the zodiac are traditionally numbered from the one in which (in Greek times) the sun is at the time of the spring equinox. By that count, Capricornus is the tenth "sign of the Zodiac."

Still another trace of Amaltheia exists in the language. Zeus took one of her horns and gave it the power of being forever filled with food and drink. This is the "horn of plenty" which is more often known by the Latin version of that phrase, the "cornucopia." The brighter stars of Capricorn (none of which are very bright) are shaped something like a cornucopia. That may be what gave the Greeks the notion in the first place of saying that it represented Amaltheia.

Another constellation connected with Zeus involves the nymph, Callisto, whom I have already mentioned. When she was in the shape of a bear, her son, Arcas, came upon her. Not knowing she was his mother, he raised his spear to kill her. Zeus, to prevent this, changed him into a bear also and then placed both in the heavens. Callisto is now the constellation of *Ursa Major,* or "the Great Bear," while Arcas is *Ursa Minor* or the "Little Bear."

The North Star is one of the stars in the constellation Ursa Minor. The Greeks knew that if one traveled northward, the North Star rose higher and higher in the skies. With it rose the two constellations of the bears. The Greek word for "bear" is "arktos" so they called the northern regions "arktikos."

We therefore speak of the area around the North Pole as the "arctic zone," and have it bounded by an imaginary line called the "arctic circle." The body of water in the arctic zone, which is frozen over with ice, is, of course, the "Arctic Ocean."

Around the South Pole is the "antarctic zone" bounded

by the "antarctic circle." The prefix "ant-" means "opposite" and the antarctic is, indeed, on the opposite side of the earth from the arctic. The frozen continent within the antarctic zone is "Antarctica," and the water about it is the "Antarctic Ocean."

There is still another trace of the Callisto myth in the sky. There is a bright star near the two bear constellations which seems forever to be watching them (sent by Hera, perhaps). This star is called "Arcturus" from Greek words meaning "to guard the bears."

On occasion, Zeus honored the animals into which he himself turned. For instance, the bull into which he turned himself to kidnap Europa was placed in the sky as "Taurus," the Latin word for "the bull." This is the second sign of the zodiac.

Of course, the original meaning of the bull might be purely practical. The sun enters Taurus in early spring and this may be taken to symbolize the time of plowing. In ancient days, oxen and bullocks were used for plowing, so you see the connection.

It may also be that the eagle, in the form of which Zeus carried off Ganymede, is honored as the constellation "Aquila" (ak'wi-luh), which is Latin for "eagle."

It might seem to you that the individual stars in these constellations might also be used to memorialize myths. Actually, most of them do not. Most stars carry Arabic names given them in the Middle Ages. Those which, like Arcturus, have names dating back to Greek and Roman times, are in the minority.

Cronus and Rhea had three daughters as well as three sons. Of these, I have mentioned Hera, who was Zeus's wife as well as his sister. She was the goddess of marriage, childbirth and women's affairs generally. The other two were *Demeter* (de-mee'-ter), the goddess of agriculture, and *Hestia* (hes'-tee-uh), the goddess of the fireplace; that is, of the home.

The daughters of Cronus are not as famous in myth as are the sons. Hera is important mainly as the wife of Zeus and Hestia is hardly ever mentioned. Demeter, as the goddess of agriculture, is involved with the older religions of the days before the Greeks came. One famous myth about her remained familiar.

Demeter had a daughter, *Persephone* (per-sef'-o-nee), who, while playing in the fields of Sicily, was carried off by Hades, who had fallen in love with her. Demeter searched for her without success for a long time and in her sorrow refused to let the ground bear grain. Mankind was faced with starvation.

Zeus then persuaded Hades to let Persephone return provided she had eaten none of the food in the underground kingdom. At the last moment, though, Hades tricked Persephone into eating four pomegranate seeds. As a result, Demeter had to allow Persephone to remain underground with Hades four months of every year, one for each seed.

While Persephone was underground, the earth bore no grain, the trees lost their leaves and even the sun scarcely shone. Only with Persephone's return, did the goddess of agriculture allow the earth to return to life.

This myth is intended to explain why winter comes each year.

Demeter was especially worshiped at a district near Athens called Eleusis (e-lyoo'sis). The myth explained it by saying that Demeter had passed through Eleusis while looking for Persephone and had been kindly treated there so that she taught them certain rites in exchange.

Actually, though, the ceremonies probably existed before the Greeks invaded the land. The Eleusinian ceremonies were not like the ordinary Olympian ones. The Olympian rites were celebrated openly and anyone who liked could join in. The Eleusinian ceremonies were secret and no one could join until he had been specially initiated.

Furthermore, one who was initiated had to swear never to reveal the rites (and no one ever did). Someone who had taken such an oath was called "mystes" from a Greek word meaning "close-mouthed." As a result, such secret rites were called "mysteries." There were a number of such "mystery religions" in ancient Greece, but of them all, the Eleusinian mysteries were the most famous.

Of course, the word "mystery" gradually weakened and came to mean anything that was secret or hidden. The most common use, nowadays, is for a book about a puzzling crime to which someone must find an ingeniously hidden solution.

The Romans identified three of their own goddesses with the three daughters of Cronus and in every case it is the Roman name that is more familiar to us today. With Hera, the Romans identified *Juno,* the wife of their Jupiter. With Demeter, they identified their goddess of agriculture, *Ceres* (see'reez). And with Hestia, they identified their goddess of the fireplace, *Vesta.* (In addition, their version of the name Persephone is *Proserpine* (pros'urpine) and that, too, is the more familiar version now.)

Some of the traces these goddesses have left are very familiar indeed. The sixth month was sacred to Juno and it is called "June" to this day. Juno (Hera) is the goddess of marriage and June is still considered the traditional month for marriage. Many girls dream of being not just a bride but a "June bride."

Ceres (Demeter) is the goddess of agriculture and particularly of grains, such as wheat, corn, rice, barley and oats. These are the most important foods in a farming society and they are called "cereals" after Ceres.

Vesta's trace is a little old-fashioned now. She was the goddess of the fireplace and when matches were first invented they seemed miniature fireplaces so, for a while, they were called "vestas."

None of these daughters of Cronus were honored among the planets known to the ancient Greeks. An opportunity to correct the situation arose in 1801, however, when a Sicilian astronomer, Giuseppi Piazzi, discovered a small planet which followed an orbit between Mars and Jupiter. It was far smaller than any planet previously known, being only 485 miles in diameter.

Ceres had always been particularly connected with Sicily, which was an important grain-growing area in Greek and Roman times. It was from Sicily that Persephone was carried away. Piazzi therefore honored his native region by suggesting that this small planet be named Ceres. The suggestion was accepted.

Once that was done, Ceres entered the table of elements, too. Klaproth, whom I have mentioned before, had a habit of naming elements after myths and especially after new planets that involved myths. In 1803, he therefore named a new element after the planet Ceres, and "cerium" joined the list.

Actually, Ceres proved to be only the first of a large number of tiny objects located between Jupiter and Mars. These are known as "asteroids" or "planetoids" or "minor planets." In 1802, a second planetoid was found; in 1804, a third; and in 1807, a fourth. No more were found for nearly forty years and then better telescopes and, eventually, the use of photography resulted in the discovery of thousands.

The use of the name Ceres originated the custom of naming all the planetoids (with certain exceptions I'll mention later) after goddesses. This gave astronomers a chance to honor all sorts of minor goddesses and nymphs.

Among the first to be honored were the daughters of Cronus. The name of Ceres was given to the first planetoid, as I've said. The third to be discovered was named "Juno" and the fourth was named "Vesta."

Although Vesta is not the largest planetoid (Ceres is), it is the brightest. It is the only planetoid that can sometimes, just barely, be made out with the naked eye, so it is well named after the goddess of the fireplace.

As for Proserpina, her name is that of the twenty-sixth planetoid to be discovered.

4 THE CHILDREN OF ZEUS

IN THE GREEK MYTHS, there were no further dethronements after Zeus established his power. The various Olympians had children but none rose in successful revolt. Instead they were peacefully allowed to enter the Olympian family and become gods and goddesses on an equal footing with the rest (although all remained under the rule of Zeus).

Probably the various children of the Olympians were originally local gods and goddesses of various native tribes who entered into alliance with the invading Greeks. In deed several gods or goddesses may have been combined under one name. For that reason, different stories that do not fit together may be told about a particular god or goddess.

For instance, there are two entirely separate stories about the birth of the goddess *Aphrodite* (a-fro-die'-tee). In one version, she is supposed to have been the daughter of Uranus and Gaea. She rose from the sea foam on a scallop shell, a sister of the Titans and far older than the Olympians.

This is probably a myth about a goddess worshiped by the people who preceded the Greeks. When the Greeks arrived, they adopted Aphrodite into the Olympian family by making her the daughter of Zeus and of the Titaness Dione.

Regardless of her origin, the Greeks considered Aphrodite the most beautiful of the goddesses. She was the goddess of beauty and love. The Romans identified their own goddess of beauty, *Venus,* with Aphrodite, and Venus is more familiar to us.

Under either name, the goddess is the prototype of beauty; that is, the original model to which everything since then must be compared. That is why when we wish to pay a high compliment to the good looks of some girl, we may call her a Venus. The Romans paid such honor to Venus that "venerate" has come to mean to honor and respect. Then, since age is respected, or should be, old men are said to be "venerable."

Venus (or Aphrodite) wore a girdle or belt, called the "cestus," which was supposed to increase her attractions and make her irresistible. A beautiful and charming woman is sometimes said to wear "Aphrodite's girdle." Zoologists spoil the poetry of that by giving the name "Venus-girdle" or "cestus" to certain flatworms living in the sea that are about a foot long and shaped just like a belt.

Venus is the one goddess whose name was given to an important planet. This is the planet commonly called the "evening star" or the "morning star" (depending on which side of the sun it happens to be). It is the brightest and most beautiful object in the heavens next to the sun and moon, and is far brighter than any star.

Originally the Greeks thought they were two different planets. They called the morning star *Phosphorus* ("lightbringer" in Greek) because once it appeared in the eastern skies, the light of dawn would soon come. The evening star was called *Hesperus* ("west" in Greek) because it always shone in the western sky after sunset.

Once the Greeks learned that Phosphorus and Hesperus were really the same planet, they named it Aphrodite as befitted its beauty. The Romans called it Venus and so do we.

Another daughter of Zeus by a Titaness is Athena. The myth has Zeus swallowing *Metis,* a Titaness who was considered his first wife. He married Hera only afterward.

Metis had a daughter within Zeus, and Zeus discovered this only after he found himself suffering from a bad headache. It was so bad that he had to have his head split open and when this was done, out sprang the goddess *Athena* (a-thee'nuh), full grown and fully armed.

This seems like a rather silly myth, but "metis" is the Greek word for "wisdom" and Athena was considered the goddess of knowledge and of the arts of both war and peace. The myth is therefore a way of saying that after Zeus came to power he absorbed wisdom, and out of the thoughts in his head arose the knowledge out of which the arts developed.

Athena was considered the goddess in particular charge of a Greek city which was named "Athenai" in her honor. In English, this city is known as "Athens." At the peak of Greek civilization, Athens was the most powerful, richest and civilized of all the Greek cities. No city has been as greatly admired by as many people as has Athens. It is still the capital of modern Greece.

Because of the reputation of Athens as a chief center of civilization, cities that consider themselves to be a center of learning still call themselves after that Greek city. Boston considers itself the "Athens of America" for instance.

One of the alternate names of Athena is *Pallas* (pal'us). One of the stories as to how she came to have this name was that at one time Athena killed a giant named Pallas and adopted his name. Probably what really happened is that a tribe worshiping a goddess named Pallas joined the Greeks and Pallas was identified with Athena. Anyway, in poetry, Athena was frequently referred to as "Pallas Athena."

In the list of the planetoids, the second one discovered (in 1802) was named Pallas. With a diameter of 304 miles, it is the second largest of the asteroids. (The ninth asteroid discovered—in 1848—was named Metis after the mother of Athena.)

Pallas entered the table of elements almost at once. In 1803, the English chemist, William Hyde Wollaston, discovered a new element. Klaproth had just named cerium after the first planetoid, Ceres, and Wollaston followed suit by naming his new element "palladium" after Pallas.

Palladium has a second meaning, too. The city of Troy (which I will talk about later in the book) had a statue of Pallas Athena which was called a "palladium." There was a tradition that Troy could not be taken as long as the palladium was inside the city. (They eventually lost the statue and Troy fell.) Nowadays, any object or tradition which is supposed to guard a nation or some cherished way of life is called a "palladium." The American constitution, for instance, can be considered the palladium of our liberties.

Some people in modern times have thought, from the sound of the word, that a palladium was an ancient circus or theater, like the Colosseum. It sometimes happens, therefore, that a movie house may be given the name. Athena is associated with the name of an actual building, though; perhaps the most beautiful building ever erected. Since Athena never married nor had any love affairs, the Greeks often called her "Athena Parthenos" ("Athena the Virgin"). When the Athenians built her a beautiful temple, completed in 437 B.C., they called it the "Parthenon." Its ruins still stand to remind us of the most glorious days of Greece.

The Romans identified their own goddess of practical arts, *Minerva* (from a Latin word meaning "mind"), with Athena. However, probably because of the fame of the city of Athens, this was one case in which the Greek name remained more familiar in modern times.

One of the sons of Zeus was *Hermes* (her'meez). His mother was *Maia*, one of the daughters of Atlas. In particular she was one of seven daughters called the *Pleiades* (plee'uh-deez.) The Pleiades were at one time pursued by a giant hunter. To rescue them, the gods changed them into doves and then set them in the skies, where they are seen as a small and pretty cluster of stars in the constellation of Taurus. One of those stars still has the name "Maia." Another is "Atlas," after the father of the Pleiades.

Although there are seven Pleiades, most people can only see six. The seventh, say the Greeks, dimmed her light in shame and grief because she fell in love with a mortal man instead of with a god. She is referred to as the "lost Pleiad."

Actually, the Pleiades are a group of stars that are far more than seven in number. We only see the very brightest with the naked eye. A field glass shows dozens and a telescope will show hundreds. Despite that, any group of exactly seven famous people is called a "Pleiad."

There is a Roman goddess called Maia also. She had nothing to do with the Greek Maia, but there is often confusion between the two. The most important thing about the Roman Maia is that the month of "May" is named after her.

As for Hermes, the son of the Greek Maia, he was considered the messenger of the gods and so was naturally imagined as very swift. He is usually pictured with wings on his sandals and on his cap. He was also the god of commerce, cunning and invention.

In later years, the Greeks adopted an Egyptian god of learning and identified him with Hermes. They called the combination "Hermes Trismegistus" ("Hermes the thrice-great"). Hermes Trismegistus was considered the god of chemical knowledge in particular, for the Egyptians had a great reputation as chemists in ancient days. (In fact, the very word "chemistry" may have come from an ancient name for Egypt.) As a result, an old-fashioned name for chemistry is the "hermetic art."

A more familiar use of the term arises from the fact that chemists often pinched closed the glass neck of a vessel to keep the contents from exposure to air. Anything that is airtight is still said to be "hermetically sealed."

In ancient times, messages from one ruler to another or between armies were carried by "heralds." These had to be treated with respect and could not be harmed. They carried a special staff as the sign of their office and this was called a "caduceus" (ka-doo'syoos). Since Hermes acted as a herald when he carried messages, he carried such a staff. Because Hermes moved so quickly, the staff, as well as his cap and sandals, carried wings.

Later, when he became Hermes Trismegistus, there was an addition to the staff. Chemistry is associated with medicine and therefore so was Hermes. (A mythical powder supposed to be capable of curing wounds when applied to them was called a "hermetic powder.") Now in ancient times, doctors were associated with snakes. This may have been because snakes had the ability to shed their skins, and seemed, to the Greeks, to be renewing their youth when they did so. This youth-renewal was what they expected or hoped for from doctors.

Because of this, the caduceus of Hermes (which may have been wreathed with olive branches to begin with) gained two snakes which coiled about it. The caduceus, complete with wings and snakes, has symbolized doctors and the profession of medicine ever since. It still forms the insignia of the United States Army Medical Corps.

Now of all the planets in the sky, the one that moves most quickly against the background of the stars was naturally named after the swift-footed Hermes. The Romans identified their own god of commerce, *Mercury*, with Hermes, and so we know the planet as Mercury.

Zeus had twin children of whom still another Titaness, *Leto* (lee'toe), was the mother. The Romans called her *Latona* (la-toe'nuh) and she is better known by that name.

The jealous Hera refused to allow Leto rest on any land in order to have the children. However, Leto fled to Delos, the smallest island in the Aegean Sea. This was a floating island so it didn't count as land. After the birth of the twins, *Apollo* (a-pol'-o) and *Artemis* (ar'te-mis), Delos was fixed to the sea bottom and floated no more.

Because they were born on Mount Cynthus on the island, the twins were occasionally called *Cynthius* and *Cynthia*.

Both are pictured as youthful archers. Apollo is the ideal of manly beauty, so that a very handsome man might be called an "Apollo." He is also the god of poetry and music. The Romans had no equivalent for Apollo and they adopted him under that name.

Artemis is the goddess of the hunt. The Romans identified a forest goddess, *Diana,* with Artemis, and it is as Diana that she is most familiar to us.

Now the mother of Leto was the Titaness Phoebe (who was honored as the eighth satellite of Saturn). Phoebe, whose name in Greek means "the shining one," was probably a goddess of either the moon or the sun in the days before the Greeks. The Greeks forced this into their own system of myths by making Apollo and Artemis the grandchildren of Phoebe and letting them rule the sun and moon.

Apollo was considered the god of the sun and even took over a masculine version of Phoebe's name. He was frequently called "Phoebus Apollo" or just "Phoebus" (fee'-bus). Artemis (and, therefore, the Roman Diana as well) was the goddess of the moon. This is another example in which the Olympians replaced the Titans, Apollo replacing Helios and Artemis replacing Selene. However, until the very end, the Greeks talked of Helios and Selene as well as of Apollo and Artemis, so the replacement wasn't perfect.

The arrows of Apollo and Artemis invariably killed and the Greeks explained epidemics of disease by supposing that the children of Leto were shooting at people right and left. Naturally, by praying to Apollo, the epidemic might be made to stop. In this way, Apollo became associated with the cure of disease.

This led to a myth in which Apollo was thought to have had a son *Asclepius* (as-klep'ee-us), who is better known under the Roman version of the name, *Aesculapius* (es'kyoo-lay'pee-us). He was the god of medicine and healing, eventually, but at first he was considered a merely human doctor. However, he was such a good doctor that he never lost a patient and, in fact, he could raise the dead back to life.

Hades complained about losing business and to keep peace in the family, Zeus killed Asclepius with a thunderbolt. After his death, he was made a god. He was also placed among the constellations, where he is pictured as a man holding a serpent in his hands. The serpent, as I explained earlier in the chapter, is a symbol of medicine and doctors. The Latin name of the constellation is "Ophi-uchus" (oh-fee-oo'kus) which means "serpent-holder." Sometimes the stars forming the serpent are referred to as a separate constellation called "Serpens" ("serpent") and occasionally the whole constellation is referred to as "Serpentarius."

You might wonder if any of the children of Zeus had Hera for a mother. The answer is yes. *Ares* (ay'reez) was the son of Zeus and Hera. He is the cruel and bloody god of war, who delighted in battle. When he went into battle, his sons, *Phobos* (foe'bus) and *Deimos* (die'mus), prepared his chariot. Since "phobos" is the Greek word for "fear" and "deimos" for "terror," this is just a way of saying that war is attended by fear and terror.

Phobos leaves his mark in modern psychology, for a "phobia" is any abnormal fear. "Claustrophobia" is the abnormal fear of closed places, for instance, and "agoraphobia" is the abnormal fear of wide open spaces. A certain disease affects the nerves so that the sufferer falls into convulsions if he tries to drink. It is therefore called "hydrophobia" ("fear of water") because the Greeks thought the convulsions were due to a fear of water instead of to a virus, as we now know they are.

It seems natural that the Greeks named the fourth planet after Ares, since the fourth planet shines with a ruddy color, resembling blood. That is fit for the god of war.

The Romans identified their god of war, *Mars,* with Ares, so we know the planet as Mars. Originally, Mars was one of the most important of the Roman gods and an entire month of the year was dedicated to him. We still call the third month "March" in his honor.

It wasn't until 1877 that the planet Mars was found to have any satellites. In that year, the American astronomer Asaph Hall discovered two of them. They were very tiny, being only five or ten miles in diameter, but they were satellites. Hall named them "Phobos" and "Deimos" so that in the heavens, as in the myths and in reality, war is accompanied by fear and terror.

The Greek name, Ares, still leaves its trace in the sky. There is a bright red star, of the same color as Mars and almost as bright. This star is called "Antares" (an-tay'reez), which means "opposite to Mars" or balancing it, as on a seesaw.

Actually the balance is very poor, because Mars is a rather small planet only a little over 4000 miles in diameter and only about 1/9 as massive as the earth. Antares, on the other hand, is one of the largest stars known, a giant red star far, far larger than our sun.

The planet Venus has no satellites. Nevertheless, mythical characters associated with Venus (or Aphrodite, rather) did get their chance. That chance first came in 1898, when the German astronomer G. Witt discovered a new planetoid, the 433rd to be discovered.

He found that although all the planetoids then known had orbits that lay between Mars and Jupiter, this one did not. Its orbit lay between Mars and the earth. Its orbit approached that of the earth more closely than did the orbits of either Mars or Venus which were otherwise our closest planetary neighbors. Witt therefore looked for a name that would go with both Mars (Ares) and Venus (Aphrodite).

It so happens that Ares and Aphrodite were pictured as having a young son named *Eros* (ee'ros). He is the young god of love and is pictured as a child with a bow and arrow. When one of his arrows strikes a heart, that person falls in love. Sometimes he is shown blindfolded to indicate that young people may fall in love blindly. The fact that Eros is supposed to be the child of Ares and Aphrodite may be the Greek way of saying that beautiful women are particularly attracted to soldiers, and vice versa. Perhaps so. We have a saying, "Only the brave deserve the fair."

Anyway, we still have Eros on Valentine cards and in cartoons. We also see hearts with arrows through them to indicate love. We know Eros better by the equivalent Roman name of *Cupid*. Both names have left traces. Anything which arouses feelings of romantic love is said to be "erotic." However, there are other types of love, too. Thus, the Roman name of the little god of love is to be found in the word "cupidity" which describes too much love of money or material things.

So Witt named his new little asteroid (it is only 15 miles through in its longest direction) "Eros." This started a fashion of naming planetoids which followed unusual orbits, outside the space between Mars and Jupiter, with masculine names.

During the twentieth century, other small asteroids have been found which approach the earth more closely than either Mars or Venus. Some have received other names connected with Aphrodite. One is "Anteros" ("opposite to Eros") and another is called "Amor," which is another Latin word for "love."

Then there is one called "Adonis" after a young man with whom Aphrodite had been in love. He was pictured as so handsome, that a good-looking man is still referred to as an "Adonis" as well as an Apollo.

Two others have been named "Apollo" and "Hermes." Hermes is a very remarkable little planetoid in that it can sometimes approach within 200,000 miles of the earth. This is closer than any other visible body can approach. It is an even closer approach than our own moon can manage.

Another child of Hera's was *Hephaestus* (he-fes'tus). He was an exceptional god in that he had a physical deformity, for he was lame. One story to account for this was that Hera dropped him from Olympus in shame because he was weakly at birth. Another is that Zeus threw him from heaven because he sided with his mother during one of her quarrels with Zeus. In either case, he fell all the way from heaven to earth, and was lame as a result.

He was the god of smiths and was always pictured working at his forge. He was the only god shown working with his hands.

The Romans had a god of fire and forge themselves, whom they pictured as working in the depths of Mount Etna, the great Sicilian volcano. The Romans called this god *Vulcan* and identified him with Hephaestus. Vulcan is much the more familiar name to us. For one thing, all mountains that, like Mount Etna, belch fire and flame are now called "volcanoes."

Another trace of the name is to be found in a matter concerning rubber. In the first part of the 1800's, attempts were made to use rubber in waterproof clothing. Unfortunately, the rubber got soft and sticky in warm weather and hard and leathery in cold weather. Chemists tried to find ways to prevent this.

In 1839, an American inventor named Charles Goodyear discovered by accident that if rubber and sulfur were heated together, the rubber became dry and flexible in both hot and cold weather. In this way, rubber could finally be put to many practical uses. The process by which this was done involved the use of heat. Consequently, such rubber was said to be "vulcanized."

However, the most dramatic episode in the history of the name of the god of the smiths came shortly after the discovery of vulcanization. The planet Mercury had a very small unevenness in its path of travel about the sun which astronomers could not account for.

In 1845, Leverrier, who was in the process of working out the position of the soon-to-be-discovered planet Neptune, tackled this problem also. He thought there might be a planet even closer to the sun than Mercury was. Its gravitational pull might be tugging at Mercury and that would account for the unevenness in its motion.

Such a planet would be closer to the fire of the sun than any other would be. It would be like a smith working at the very forge of the solar system. Leverrier therefore suggested that the new planet be called "Vulcan."

However, although astronomers searched for Vulcan for many years they could never find it. Then, in 1915, Albert Einstein advanced a new theory which explained perfectly the unevenness in Mercury's motion. There was no need for any new planet and so it turned out that the planet Vulcan did not exist after all.

I have now described the origin of the names of all the major planets of the solar system. Before leaving the planets, however, I would like to describe some ways in which they continued to spread the traces of myth even farther.

For instance, long before the days of modern astronomy, symbols were invented to represent the different planets. These involved some reference to the god, and since the symbols are still used today, the traces of myth remain.

Thus, the symbol of the planet Mercury is ☿, which is a crude picture of the caduceus, with the two serpents twining and the wings on top. The symbol of Venus is ♀, which is a looking glass, surely a natural object to connect with a goddess of beauty.

The symbol of Mars is ♂, which is supposed to be a shield and spear, suitable for the god of war.

It is more difficult to work out the meaning of ♃, which is the symbol of Jupiter. Some think it is a crude picture of an eagle with its wings outstretched. An eagle was one of the creatures into which Zeus turned himself on his adventures.

The symbol for Saturn is ♄, the scythe with which Cronus defeated his father, Uranus.

Of the planets discovered in modern times, Uranus and Pluto have modern symbols, involving letters of the alphabet. The symbol of Nepture, however, is ♆. This symbolizes the special three-pronged spear which Poseidon used to control the waves. It is called a "trident" (trie′dent) from Latin words meaning "three teeth."

Two of these symbols are used in fields other than astronomy. When a scientist is tracing the line of descent of some man or animal, in order to determine the manner in which certain traits are inherited, he usually indicates females by the symbol for Venus (♀) and males by the symbol for Mars (♂).

The ancients felt that the seven planets (they included the sun and moon along with Mercury, Venus, Mars, Jupiter and Saturn) were particularly important in the affairs of men. A study of their position among the stars at the moment of his birth was supposed to give information about his fate. This type of study is called "astrology" and there are many people who still believe there is something in it, although scientists are certain it is complete foolishness.

The general character of a person was thought to be determined by which planet he was "born under," according to the calculations of astrologers, and there are traces of this superstition in our language, still.

For instance, the planet Mercury moves faster among the stars than does any other planet. A person born "under Mercury" would therefore have to be quick-witted and changeable, lively and gay. This is what is meant by the word "mercurial." On the other hand, those born under Saturn, the slow-moving planet, are heavy, gloomy and dull, and this is what is meant by the word "saturnine."

Someone born under Mars would be warlike, of course, or "martial." More surprising is the fact that those born under Jupiter are thought to be happy people. It is for this reason that the adjective "jovial" mean joyous.

As for the moon, it was thought to have an unsettling effect on people's minds. To be out in the light of the full moon would lead to madness, people suspected. This is just superstition, but the language still has words like "moon-mad," "moon-sick" and "moon-struck," all meaning "crazy," while a "moon-calf" is a fool.

A more dignified word for "crazy" is "lunatic" but that comes from Luna, the Roman goddess of the moon. And it has been shortened in common speech to the not so dignified "loonies."

Each of the seven planets was also supposed to have a special day of the week in its charge, as follows: First day (Sol or the sun); Second day (Luna or the moon); Third day (Mars); Fourth day (Mercury); Fifth day (Jupiter); Sixth day (Venus) and Seventh day (Saturn).

The days of the week were named after the planets in the Latin language. These names held on in the languages closely related to Latin. For instance, in French, the second, third and fourth days of the week are "lundi," "mardi," and "mercredi."

In English, however, all the days of the week but the seventh are named after Norse gods, which were worshiped by the Anglo-Saxons before their conversion to Christianity. The Norse gods corresponded to the planets in a rough sort of way, however. For instance, the first and second days of the week, in English, are "Sunday" and "Monday." It is the seventh day that is the clear case, however. For some reason, it retained the Latin name of "Saturday"—"Saturn's day."

The alchemists of the Middle Ages noticed that there were seven planets and seven metals. They matched up heavenly objects and metals and, as a result, additional traces of mythical characters are to be found in chemistry.

The seven metals known to the alchemists were (in English): gold, silver, copper, iron, tin, lead, and quicksilver.

Because of their colors, gold was matched with the sun and silver with the moon. The third most valuable metal was copper so that was matched with Venus, the third brightest object in the heavens.

Iron, which made the weapons of war, was naturally matched with Mars, while lead, the heavy, dull metal, was matched with Saturn, the heavy, dull planet. On the other hand, quicksilver was liquid and moved about easily, so it was matched with the quick-moving planet, Mercury. That left tin, which was matched with the remaining planet, Jupiter.

Naturally, most of this vanished as chemists grew to know more of the subject. For one thing, many more metals were discovered, and though some new metals continued to be named after new planets, most were not.

In only one case did alchemists actually succeed in changing the name of an element to the name of a planet. Quicksilver is known as "mercury" these days.

In the other cases only occasional traces remain. The best-known example is the compound silver nitrate, which still carries the old-fashioned name of "lunar caustic." The "caustic," from a Greek word meaning "biting," refers to the fact that it is related to nitric acid, a strong and biting substance. The "lunar" refers to the fact that silver is involved.

Then there is a bright-red compound of lead and oxygen which is commonly known as "red lead." It is still, however, sometimes referred to as "Saturn red" because of its content of lead, the Saturnian metal. There is also a whole series of iron compounds of different colors which have old-fashioned names involving Mars, the planet matched with iron: Mars yellow, Mars brown, Mars orange, Mars violet and so on.

But there the influence of the medieval alchemist ends. The modern chemist has shaken himself free almost entirely.

5 DEMIGODS AND MONSTERS

THERE ARE any number of minor characters among the gods and goddesses of the Greek myths. Some of these are referred to as "demigods" ("half-gods"). These are usually less powerful than gods but more powerful than human beings. Sometimes they are mortal to begin with but become gods after they die. Asclepius is one example to which I have already referred.

One god who was in the top rank of demigods was *Dionysus* (die′o-nie′sus). He was originally a god of agriculture, who was made the center of a mystery religion. The important thing about him was that he was killed but brought back to life, just as Persephone went down to Hades and returned. In all mystery religions, death and rebirth plays a part because that symbolizes the death of vegetation in the winter and its rebirth in the spring.

Later on, Dionysus was known by the name of *Bacchus* (bak′us). Celebrations in his honor were called "Dionysia" or "Bacchanalia." They were very wild and usually involved women, who were called "Bacchantes." The word "bacchanalia" now refers to any wild celebration, while any woman overcome with emotion to the point of madness is called a "bacchante."

Dionysus grew so popular that he was adopted into the Olympian family. The Greek mythmakers had him the son of Zeus, while his mother was a mortal woman named *Semele* (sem'uh-lee). Probably Semele was herself an earth goddess originally who played a part in the Bacchanalia.

A lesser god is *Pan,* supposed to be a son of Hermes. Pan is a god of fields and woods, a spirit of all nature in fact, and that may be where he gets his name, for it is a Greek word meaning "all." Pan is described as having the hindquarters and legs plus the ears and horns of a goat, which shows his connection with animal life.

He is usually pictured as dancing happily while he plays on a simple instrument, made up of a series of hollow tubes or reeds of different lengths. Such an instrument is still called a "Pan pipe," or the "pipes of Pan."

Pan obtained this instrument as follows: He fell in love with a water nymph. She ran from him and he pursued. She prayed for escape to the gods, who turned her into a reed at the riverside. Sadly, Pan cut the reeds and made the first pipes out of them. The name of the nymph was *Syrinx,* which is a Greek word meaning "pipe," and the pipes of Pan are still sometimes called a "syrinx."

The poor nymph leaves her traces in connection with another form of music. The windpipe in song-birds has a special region shaped for the production of their songs. This section is also called the "syrinx."

Less musical are those pipes through which water can be forced out of a water reservoir, or up which water can be sucked into a water reservoir. These are called "syringes," which is only the plural form of "syrinx."

Another case of a nymph running from a god was that of *Daphne* (daf'nee), who ran from Apollo and escaped only by being turned into a laurel tree. The genus of plants to which the laurel belongs is called "Daphne" by botanists, and "daphnean" means "bashful" or "shy."

The early Christians thought of Pan and of other woodland spirits as particularly immoral, and they began to describe the devil in the shape of Pan. The modern picture of the devil, with his horns, hoofs and tail, is just poor old Pan made wicked.

The Romans had a similar nature god, *Faunus*, whom they identified with Pan. Faunus was a god of animal life in particular and had a sister named *Flora*, who was the goddess of flowers and of plant life in general. These names are now applied to animal and plant life, so that biologists will speak of the "fauna" (animal life) and "flora" (plant life) of a particular region. Flora's name was also given to the eighth planetoid to be discovered. (The word "fawn," meaning a young deer, is from the Anglo-Saxon and has no connection with Faunus.)

The Roman goddess of fruit trees, in particular, among the plants was *Pomona* (puh-moe'nuh) and so the Latin word "pomum" means "fruit." From that we have "pome" meaning a juicy, fleshy fruit like that of the apple, and "pomegranate," which is a fruit containing grains and with the outer appearance of an apple. There is also "pomade" which is a kind of ointment that has apples as one of its ingredients, and a small box to carry such an ointment is a "pomander." The thirty-second planetoid is named Pomona.

As an example of a minor goddess there is *Iris,* who, like Hermes, but on a lower level, served as a messenger of the gods. She specialized in bearing messages from the gods to human beings and to do this she had frequently to descend from heaven to earth. The logical stairway by which this might be done was the rainbow and, indeed, "iris" is the Greek word for rainbow.

The most remarkable thing about the rainbow is its many colors, of course, so the word "iris" has come to be applied to other many-colored objects. For instance, as we all know, human eyes come in different shades of color. In 1721, a Danish naturalist, Jakob Benignus Winslow, called the colored part of the eye the "iris" and the name has been kept. It is also applied to the flag, a plant with large flowers that come in a variety of colors.

The plural form of "iris" in the Greek is "irides" and

the "d" shows up in several other English words. For instance, thin films such as those of oil on water, soap bubbles, mother-of-pearl and so on, show a play of colors that changes as the line of sight is shifted. This is called "iridescence."

And in 1803, an English chemist named Smithson Tennant discovered a new element which combined with other elements to form substances of various colors. In honor of the many colors, he named the element "iridium."

An even more pleasant example of the minor goddess, this time a whole group of them, are the *Muses*. These were pictured as nine beautiful girls, the daughters of Zeus. The mother was the Titaness *Mnemosyne* (nemos'i-nee). The name, in Greek, means "memory" and this survives today, most commonly, in the word "mnemonic" meaning anything that pertains to memory and particularly something that aids the memory (such as the little verse "Thirty days hath September . . .").

The Muses themselves are the goddesses of the various fine arts. (In modern times, we might consider them the goddesses of "show business.") They were particularly the goddesses of poetic inspiration and poets of ancient times and even of early modern times would always start important poems by calling upon the Muses for inspiration. Since poetry before the days of writing had to be memorized, it is not surprising that the Muses, who represent poetic inspiration, were considered the daughters of memory (Mnemosyne).

Furthermore, since poetry, drama and the other forms of recitation in ancient times were always done to the accompaniment of melodious sound, it is not surprising that this melodious sound should be termed "music."

Temples built in honor of the Muses were dedicated to learning and study and such temples were known as "museums." The word is used today a little differently. It refers to buildings used for the collection of objects of interest in some art or science.

Each of the nine Muses was eventually pictured as in charge of a different branch of fine art. The usual listing has *Calliope* (ka-lie'o-pee) as chief of the Muses. Her name comes from Greek words meaning "beautiful voice." She was the Muse of eloquence and heroic poetry. Her name is now used for an instrument made of a series of steam whistles. We are used to hearing it played in a circus parade and on merry-go-rounds. However, although it is lively and cheerful, it is not exactly a "beautiful voice."

Clio (klie'o), meaning "to tell of," was the Muse of history. *Erato* (er'a-toe) and Urania (yoo-ray'-nee-uh) are two Muses with names that are feminine forms of Eros and Uranus. Erato is naturally the Muse of love poetry and Urania is the Muse of astronomy, since "eros" means "love" and "uranus" means "sky."

Euterpe (yoo-ter'pee), meaning "to delight well," is the Muse of ordinary music, while *Polyhymnia* (pol'ee-hym'nee-uh) is the Muse of religious music. The name of that Muse means "many hymns" and "hymn" is still used, of course, for any song on a religious subject.

Thalia (tha-lie'uh), meaning "blooming," is the Muse of comedy, while *Melpomene* (mel-pom'i-nee), meaning "to sing," is the Muse of tragedy.

Finally, *Terpsichore* (terp-sik'o-ree) is the Muse of the dance. For some reason, this name hangs on and dancing is sometimes spoken of, in a joking sort of way, as the "terpsichorean art."

Three of the early planetoids to be discovered were named after various muses. Planetoid number eighteen was named Melpomene; planetoid number twenty-two was named Calliope, and planetoid number twenty-three was named Thalia. All three planetoids were discovered in 1852.

Another pleasant group of sisters are three who are known as "Gratiae" in Latin. They are the goddesses of all that is charming in women and, of course, the English version of the Latin name is "the three *Graces*." We are all familiar with words like "graceful" and "gracious."

The planetoids serve as one way in which many minor goddesses enter the modern language. I will list just a few by way of example.

Planetoid number five, *Astraea* (as-tree'uh) represents the goddess of justice, though her name is the Greek word for "stars." She was pictured as the last goddess to leave the earth at the end of the Golden Age. The Greeks visualized her as the sixth of the constellations of the zodiac, Virgo (ver'-goe) meaning "the maiden." She is usually pictured as a winged girl with a sheaf of wheat in her hand. The wheat is marked by a bright star called "Spica" which is the Latin word for a spike or ear of grain. Actually, the constellation was originally an agricultural sign. When it first appears at sunset, it means the time of planting of grain is near.

Planetoid number six is *Hebe* (hee'buh). The word means "youth" and Hebe is the goddess of youth and the cupbearer of the gods, until Ganymede arrived to take over the job.

Planetoid number ten: *Hygeia* (hi-jee'uh), the daughter of Asclepius and the goddess of health, her name meaning "health." We use the word "hygiene" today to mean the study of methods for preserving health. Another daughter of Asclepius was *Panacea* (pan'a-see'uh) a word meaning "all-cure" in Greek. The word is still used today for anything supposed to be an easy cure for many difficult problems.

The Roman goddess of health, whom the Romans identified with Hygeia, was *Salus* (say'lus). For this reason, the word "salutary" means "healthful." Furthermore, when we greet someone, we usually wish him or her good health or imply that we do by asking after their well-being. "How are you?" we usually say. Therefore, a greeting is a "salutation" or a "salute."

A minor Roman god should also be mentioned in connection with the name of one of the months, which are all Latin in origin.

I have already mentioned March (Mars), May (Maia) and June (Juno). But then there is a month involving *Janus* (jay'nus) who was the Roman god of doors, to begin with. He therefore became the god who presided over beginnings (entrance through a door) and endings (exit by a door). He was usually pictured with two faces, one looking forward and one backward.

The first month of the year is a time for beginning a new year and ending the old. We still celebrate it as a time for looking sentimentally at the past and hopefully toward the future. So it is named for Janus and called "January." And, of course, a man who is in charge of the doors of a building and of other parts of it, as well, is a "janitor."

The names of the remaining months are not mythical in origin.

The Romans, in fact, had any number of minor mythical characters, each governing some single part of life. They had a goddess who was in charge of a baby's first step, another in charge of its first tooth and so on. They had special gods or spirits in charge of a particular place and even of each particular person. The Romans called this personal spirit a *genius*.

Whatever made a person individual, and different from other persons, was referred to as his genius. When a particular person was far above other people in intelligence, brilliance or creative ability, his genius seemed in special charge because a mere man could not be that good without a little supernatural help. He was more the guiding spirit itself than a man. In fact, he was a "genius."

The Greek word for the spirit possessing and guiding the individual was *daimon*. Since to the early Christians any kind of spirit possessing a human being was evil, the word, which in English is "demon," came to mean a kind of devil.

The imaginative Greeks did not confine themselves to gods and demigods. They also dreamed up a variety of monsters of all types. Some, of course, were monstrous mainly because of their size. I have already mentioned the Gigantes, Cyclops and Titans.

After Zeus had defeated the Titans and established himself as ruler of the universe there were occasional revolts, all unsuccessful. (This may be a reflection of revolts of the conquered pre-Greeks against the Greek invaders.)

The story of the revolt of the Gigantes (giants) was used by the mythmakers as a chance to go to extremes. For instance, Athena killed the giant *Enceladus* (en-sel'a-dus) by crushing him under a rock so large that it lay there in the Mediterranean as the island of Sicily. The mythmakers also had the various Olympians use their specialties in winning the battle. For instance, Hephaestus managed to kill the giant *Mimas* (mie'mas) by pouring a ladle of molten metal over him. (It was in this same battle that Athena was supposed to have killed the giant Pallas, and taken his name.)

The modern trace of that revolt lies among Saturn's satellites. In 1789 Herschel, the discoverer of Uranus, likewise discovered satellites one and two of Saturn. These were the only ones not named after Titans. Instead, Herschel named them "Mimas" and "Enceladus" so that the giants who warred against the Olympians might join the Titans who did the same.

After that, a pair of giants named *Otus* (oh'tus) and *Ephialtes* (e'fee-al'teez) attacked Olympus. In doing so, they piled the nearby mountain of Pelion upon the mountain of Ossa in order to get a combined mountain high enough to overlook Olympus. They were eventually destroyed, but ever since, the phrase "to pile Pelion upon Ossa" has been used to describe any superhumanly difficult task.

The most dangerous revolt came next. Gaea, the goddess of the earth, annoyed at the destruction of her children, the Gigantes, brought forth the most terrible monster of all, and the largest giant who ever existed. He was named *Typhon* (tie'fon). He was hundreds of miles high and wide and his arms and legs ended in serpents.

For a while, the Olympians were completely terrified of him. For instance, Aphrodite and Eros once met up with Typhon on the banks of a stream. In fright, they jumped into the river and changed themselves into fish in order to escape. Having done so, they placed the image of the two fish in the heavens, as the twelfth sign of the zodiac, *Pisces* (pis'eez) meaning "fish."

Zeus was finally goaded into fighting Typhon. For a while it looked as though Zeus might actually be beaten and destroyed, but after a terrible fight, Zeus managed to use his thunderbolts and win.

The word Typhon was picked up from this myth (which became rather famous because of the excitement of the great fight) by the Arabs of the Middle Ages, who carried it to southeast Asia where it is now used in the form of "typhoon" as a word for the hurricane.

On one occasion, the Olympians themselves revolted against Zeus and might have won except that this time a monstrous giant came to Zeus's side. This was *Briareus* (brie-ay'ree-us), who was one of three giants pictured as having a hundred arms. The adjective "briarean" is for that reason sometimes used to picture a problem with numerous complications.

Not all giants were involved in revolts against the gods. One giant, *Orion* (oh-rie'on), was mainly a hunter. He was the giant whom I mentioned in an earlier chapter as chasing the Pleiades.

Eventually, Orion offended Apollo, who sent a scorpion to kill him. The scorpion failed but Apollo tricked Artemis into completing the job. Artemis (who loved Orion), on finding she had killed him, in grief begged Asclepius to bring him back to life. This Asclepius did and that was when Hades complained, as I said earlier, so that Zeus killed both Orion and Asclepius with thunderbolts.

Not only was Asclepius placed in the sky as a constellation (as I said earlier), but so were Orion and the scorpion. The scorpion became the eighth sign of the zodiac, Scorpio (skawr'pee-o). It is in this constellation that the bright star, Antares, which I have already mentioned, is to be found.

The constellation, *Orion*, is to be found in the heavens neighboring Taurus and on the side opposite Scorpio (as though bringing them any closer together would only renew the fight).

Near Orion, on the other side of Taurus, is the brightest star in the heavens. *Sirius* (see'ree-us). The Greeks explained its existence by saying that Orion had a hunting dog named Sirius and they made Sirius part of a constellation called, in Latin, *Canis Major* ("Great Dog").

Actually, this explanation was probably made up later. Sirius rises with the sun in midsummer and the ancients felt that its brightness added to that of the sun was what caused midsummer heat. This is not so, of course, but the hottest part of summer is still referred to as the "dog days." Sirius probably comes from a Greek word meaning "scorching" for this same reason.

Another bright star near Orion is *Procyon* (pro'-see-on), a name that comes from Greek words meaning "before the dog" because it rises a little earlier than Sirius does. The Greeks made Procyon part of another constellation called, in Latin, *Canis Minor* ("Little Dog") so that Orion has two dogs to help him face the bull.

The Greeks specialized in monsters that were part animal and part man (or, more usually, woman). For instance, the *Harpies* are pictured as having women's heads on birds' bodies. Originally, they may have been wind spirits which snatched away the souls of dying men (the word "harpy" comes from a Greek word meaning "to snatch").

Eventually, however, they were described as very filthy and foul-smelling, and greedy, too. It was not souls they wanted, but food. They would swoop down on feasting men, snatching up the food and dirtying what they could not snatch. The word is still used today to describe very greedy women.

An even more terrible type of "bird-women" were the *Gorgons,* a name coming from a Greek word meaning "terrible." Like the Harpies, they had the wings and claws of birds, but, worst of all, their hair was made up of living, writhing snakes. They were so horrible to look at that anyone seeing them was turned to stone. An ugly and terrifying woman is still called a "gorgon" today.

The best known of the three Gorgons which were supposed to exist was the youngest and most horrible. Her name was *Medusa* (me-doo'suh). She has found her way into zoology, for a jellyfish has long tentacles that writhe about in search of food, and these look like living snakes attached to a body. For that reason, such jellyfish are referred to as "medusas."

A sister of the Gorgons was *Echidna* (e-kid'nuh). She was a beautiful woman down to the waist and a horrible serpent below that. The same name has been given to a queer Australian animal, usually called the "spiny anteater." It has hair so it is a mammal, but on the other hand it lays eggs like a reptile. Because it seems a half-and-half creature, half mammal and half reptile (and so is Echidna since the woman half is a mammal and the serpent half a reptile) the spiny anteater was named the "echidna."

Echidna was the mother of most of the remaining monsters of Greek mythology, the father being Typhon.

Among the children of Echidna was a water monster named *Hydra* (hie'druh) from the Greek word for "water." It had a serpent's body with nine heads. Each time one head was cut off, two others grew in its place. For that reason, any set of evil conditions which simply gets worse every time an effort is made to cure it, is said to be "hydra-headed."

The Hydra has been placed in the heavens, for there is a long snaky string of stars stretching a quarter way around the southern rim of the zodiac which is called by that name. It is the largest constellation in the heavens but otherwise there is nothing particularly remarkable about it.

There is a harmless little animal, related to the jellyfish, and only half an inch long or so, which has a set of about half a dozen tiny tentacles with which it catches tiny bits of food. It looks like a very small many-headed creature of the water, and it is named the "fresh-water hydra."

Another child of Echidna was the *Sphinx,* a creature with a woman's head and a lion's body. This would stop travelers and propose riddles. If the traveler could not solve the riddle, the Sphinx would kill him. Any person, therefore, who is hard to understand, or who speaks in riddles is called a "sphinx."

Since a person is sometimes hardest to understand when he doesn't speak at all, "sphinx" has come to be applied particularly to people who speak very little. This fits in with the Greek derivation, which is from a word meaning "to bind tight." A ring of muscle which can close an opening tightly, such as the muscle which is used to purse the lips, is a "sphincter."

The Egyptians occasionally built statues with the heads of their kings on lion's bodies. The Greeks called these sphinxes, too. In particular, there is the "Great Sphinx," which is 172 feet long and 66 feet high. This is what most people think of when they hear the word "sphinx."

Another monstrous child of Echidna is the *Chimaera* (ki-mee'ruh), which is not merely half-and-half, but third-and-third-and-third. It is usually pictured as a fire-breathing monster with a lion's head, a goat's body (sometimes with a goat's head arising from the back) and a dragon or serpent as the tail. This is so much wilder than the usual run of imaginary monsters that the word "chimaera" has come into our language to mean any imaginary creature or, in fact, any ridiculous idea.

The word can refer to real things, too, however. Botanists can graft a part of one plant onto a second, and zoologists can sometimes do the same thing with simple animals. Such combinations are called "chimaeras." There is also an oddly shaped shark called a "chimaera."

Echidna is also the mother of Cerberus whom I have mentioned before and of the Nemean Lion which I will mention later.

A more straightforward monster, a serpent and no more, but one of gigantic and horrible size, was called *Python*. Apollo killed it with his arrows and was therefore sometimes called "Apollo Pythius" (just as Athena became Pallas Athena). At the spot where the slaying took place, Apollo established the oracle of Delphi.

Actually, Pytho seems to have been the earlier name of Delphi and the myth of Apollo and Python may just signify that the Greek god Apollo had ousted an earlier goddess of the pre-Greek inhabitants. Not all traces of the earlier goddess were removed. The priestess who gave out the oracles was still called the "pythoness" and the athletic games celebrated at Delphi every four years (which were next to the Olympian games in importance) were called the "Pythian games."

In modern times zoology mirrors the myth, for we call the very largest living snakes, the boas and anacondas, "pythons."

Less horrible are the *Centaurs* (sen'tawrs), which are pictured as half man and half horse. The notion of such creatures arose, possibly, when people without horses first met up with a raiding party of mounted men. Never having seen men riding horses before, they could easily decide, in their terror, that horse and man were a single creature.

The Centaurs are usually pictured as wild, uncouth creatures, rude and uncivilized, fighting with bow and arrows. One of them, however, *Chiron* (kie′ron), was an exception. He was noble, gentle and wise, and taught medicine to many of the Greek heroes, even to Asclepius.

After his death, Chiron was placed among the constellations as the ninth sign of the zodiac, *Sagittarius* (saj′i-tay′re-us), from the Latin word for "archer." The constellation is often pictured as a centaur, drawing a bow in the act of shooting an arrow.

Now the Greeks and other ancient people only formed constellations in that part of the sky which they could see, naturally. The stars which are high in the sky at the South Pole are never visible from such lands as Egypt, Babylonia and Greece. It was only when Europeans started sailing southward along the coast of Africa in the 1400's that these stars were seen by northern eyes.

Eventually, astronomers divided these newer stars into constellations. Some of these were drawn up into imaginary pictures of rather modern objects such as Microsopium ("the microscope") and Telescopium ("the telescope"). Others, however, were given names in the mythological tradition. One large southern constellation was named *Centaurus*.

Far from being horrible, some of the Greek monsters were quite attractive. For instance there were the *Sirens,* who were usually pictured as very beautiful young women, who rested on the rocks of a seashore and sang in heavenly voices. Sailors passing near would be attracted and would steer their boats nearer, only to meet death upon the rocks.

This is probably the Greek way of symbolizing dangerous stretches of seashore which seem to invite sailors and their ships with their peaceful and harmless appearance only to destroy them with rocks hidden below the water.

In modern language, a flirtatious woman who delights in making those men who fall in love with her miserable is called a "siren." Anything which attracts men away from their duty with deceiving promise, is called a "siren song."

A "siren" sometimes refers to a sweet singer, but more often it refers to a device which sends out a thin, piercing scream that rises and falls in pitch. It is used as a warning signal attached to police cars and fire engines, but it is certainly not the beautiful song of the mythological sirens.

The Sirens may originally have been wind spirits carrying off the souls of the dead, as the Harpies originally were. Sometimes the Sirens, like the Harpies, were pictured with birds' bodies. However, since the Sirens were always associated with the sea, they eventually began to be pictured as creatures who were women down to the waist and fish below that. In other words, they became "mermaids."

Because of this, the Sirens entered zoology in a rather queer way. There are certain sea mammals called sea cows who have a habit of sticking their heads and shoulders above water and holding their young clasped to them with one arm just as a mother might hold a baby. Their hindquarters end in a flipper. Sailors seeing them at a distance, first with their babies in a human pose, then with the flipper exposed as they dived, thought they saw a mermaid.

Because of this grotesque error, the group of animals of which the sea cow is a member (which are actually very ugly and not the least like Sirens) are called "Sirenia."

Still, if these creatures are not as beautiful as the original Sirens, neither are they as dangerous. They are, in fact, entirely harmless, and a sailor would be far luckier to meet a sirenian than a Siren, however things might seem just at first.

6 TALES OF MEN

THE GREEKS did not do a great deal in their myths as far as the creation of man was concerned. The nearest thing to such an account involves the Titan, *Prometheus* (pruh-mee'thyoos). His name comes from Greek words meaning "forethought," and he had a brother, *Epimetheus* (ep'i-mee'thyoos) whose name meant "hindthought." In other words, Prometheus was wise, seeing the results of actions in advance, while Epimetheus was foolish, understanding results only after they had come about.

Both were the sons of the Titan Iapetus, and therefore brothers of Atlas. However, when the Titans and Olympians were at war, with Atlas leading the Titans, Prometheus, foreseeing that the Olympians would win, abandoned the Titans and persuaded Epimetheus to do likewise. As a result these two brothers were spared the punishment that fell on the Titans generally.

After the war with the Titans was over, men were created by Prometheus at the order of Zeus. Or, as some versions have it, ordinary mortal human beings were the descendants of Prometheus and Epimetheus.

In either case, Zeus, who did not entirely trust Prometheus, disliked men, while Prometheus, on his part, did his best to help men against the Olympians. When Zeus tried to destroy mankind with a huge flood, Prometheus managed to warn one man, *Deucalion* (dyoo-kay'lee-on), supposedly the son of Prometheus, according to some of the mythmakers. Deucalion built a ship in which he and his wife, *Pyrrha* (pir'uh), supposedly a daughter of Epimetheus, escaped.

As mankind struggled back from that catastrophe, they were neglected by the Olympians and allowed to live lives of misery and savagery. Prometheus took pity on the men he had created, or fathered, and taught them various arts and sciences that might help them to an easier life. To top things off, he stole fire from the sun and taught mankind how to use it. (This may indicate that he was the pre-Greek god of fire, replaced by Hephaestus after the Greek invasion.)

All this was in defiance of Zeus, so that any act which is very daring and defiant, or very original and creative, is called "promethean."

In revenge, Zeus created a beautiful woman to whom all the gods gave gifts of beauty, grace, wit, melody and so on. She was called *Pandora* (pan-daw'ruh) from Greek words meaning "all-gifted." She was then given to Epimetheus for a wife. Because of her beauty, Epimetheus accepted her although Prometheus had warned him against taking any gift from Zeus.

Along with Pandora, Epimetheus received a box which Pandora was forbidden to open. However, she was a true woman. At her first opportunity, she opened the box to see what was in it and out flew the spirits of old age, death, famine, sickness, grief, and all the other ills that plague human beings. Only hope was left at the bottom of the box and, when finally let out, was all that kept human beings alive under the weight of their misery.

Thus, anything which is harmless when undisturbed, but which lets loose many troubles when interfered with, is called a "Pandora's box."

Not satisfied with having his revenge on humanity, Zeus also punished Prometheus directly. He chained him to a rock in the Caucasus Mountains which, to the ancient Greeks, represented the eastern end of the world. There he was continually tortured by an eagle.

The story of Pandora is actually a moral tale, a kind of fable intended to teach men how to behave. For instance, Epimetheus is a warning against careless action taken without due consideration of possible consequences. Pandora herself is a warning against foolish curiosity.

Many mythical warnings were against the kind of pride which made people consider themselves above the law. Such pride led to insolent behavior and a disregard of the rights of others. In the Greek myths, it usually involved defying the gods—the sort of pride the Greeks called "hubris."

When that happened, the gods saw to it that the proud individual was dealt with by *Nemesis,* the goddess of retribution. The name comes from Greek words meaning to "distribute." In other words, Nemesis sees to it that matters are distributed evenly. If a person has so much good fortune that he becomes boastful, proud and insolent, she sees to it that he has a corresponding amount of bad fortune to even things out.

Since most of the Greek myths involve matters evened out by bad fortune, rather than by good fortune, "nemesis" has come to mean, in our language, an unavoidable doom.

Pride is still considered the most serious of the seven deadly sins. It was through pride that Lucifer fell, according to our own stories. We still have this old Greek feeling about pride when we speak of "the jealous gods" who won't allow anyone to be too lucky. That is why we say that "pride goeth before a fall" and why we knock wood when we talk about how fortunate we are, or how well off. That is supposed to keep off Nemesis.

An example of such a pride-goeth-before-a-fall myth is the story of *Arachne* (uh-rak'ne). She was a girl of the kingdom of Lydia (in western Asia Minor) who was very skilled at weaving. She was so proud of her skill that she boasted that even Athena, the goddess of the practical arts, including that of weaving, could do no better, and challenged Athena to a contest. (There was hubris.)

Athena accepted the challenge and both wove tapestries. Athena wove into hers all sorts of glorious stories about the gods while Arachne wove into hers unflattering stories about them. Arachne's work was excellent but Athena's was perfect. In anger at Arachne's subject matter, Athena tore Arachne's weaving to shreds and Arachne, struck with terror, hanged herself. (There was nemesis.)

Athena, who was not a cruel goddess, didn't want things to go that far, so she loosened the rope and changed Arachne into a spider. As a spider, Arachne continued spinning threads and weaving beautiful webs, and she also continues to hang from a strand of gossamer as though still trying to hang herself. Of course "arachne" is the Greek word for "spider" and the idea of the myth surely came from watching spiders at work. But it does teach a moral: avoid hubris.

In zoology, the name of the girl lives on, since spiders and their relatives are put in the class "Arachnida."

Furthermore, anything as filmy and delicate as a spider's web is said to be "arachnoid." For instance, the brain and spinal cord are enclosed by a double membrane for protection. In between the two parts of the double membrane is a third membrane which is very thin and filmy. This is called the "arachnoid membrane."

Another example of this sort of myth is that of *Phaëthon* (fay'uh-thon), the mortal son of Helios. He was so proud of being the son of the sun god, that he felt he could drive the sun (which was pictured as a gleaming chariot drawn by wild, gleaming horses) across the sky. He tricked his father into promising to let him do so. (That was hubris.)

Phaëthon drove the sun but found he could not control the horses, which went out of their course and swooped too near the earth. The Greeks supposed the burning sands of the Sahara showed where the swooping sun chariot had scorched the earth and felt that the dark color of the African natives was also the result of it. To save the earth from destruction, Zeus was forced to kill Phaëthon with a thunderbolt. (That was nemesis.)

The word "phaeton" (usually without the "h" and pronounced "fay'uh-ten") can be applied to any reckless driver. The word was also applied to a carriage or automobile without top or sides. These were light vehicles, you see, that could be driven more quickly than ordinary heavier ones. Both uses are out of date, now.

One case of hubris and nemesis struck father and daughter separately. It begins with *Tantalus*, a mortal son of Zeus, He was a great favorite of his father and the other gods. He was even allowed to join the banquets of the god and eat *ambrosia* (am-broe'zhee-a) and drink *nectar* (nek'ter). This is the food of the gods. "Ambrosia" comes from a Greek word meaning "immortal" and "nectar" from one meaning "death-defeating." As a result of such food, the veins of gods are filled with *ichor* (eye'kor) instead of blood, so that the gods are immortal.

Nowadays, in more practical times, nectar and ambrosia are used to describe any delightful food. Nectar, particularly, can refer to any sweet liquid. The sugary fluid in flowers, used by bees to make honey, is called nectar, for instance. A type of smooth-skinned peach has been named "nectarine" for its sweet taste.

To return to Tantalus, however— He felt so puffed up at the gods' friendship that he acted as though this food and drink were his in actual fact and took some back to earth with him to give to his friends. Furthermore, he boasted about this.

Nemesis followed. He was killed by Zeus and condemned to a special torture in Tartarus, one which involved food and drink. He was forced to stand forever in water up to his neck. Every time he bent to drink, however, the water sank downward and swirled away. When he stood up, the water rose to his neck again. Meanwhile, delicious fruit dangled near his face, but when he reached out for it, the wind blew it out of his reach. Thus, with food and drink continually near, he suffered eternal hunger and thirst.

For this reason, we have the word "tantalize" referring to any action which is designed to give someone false hope which is snatched away just as it seems on the point of coming true. In the same way, a glass cabinet in which bottles of wine may be locked away is called a "tantalus" because the wine can be seen but, without the key, cannot be touched.

In 1814, the tantalized Tantalus entered the list of elements. Twelve years earlier, a Swedish chemist named Anders Gustaf Eckeberg discovered a new metal. Strong acids did not affect it. It could stand in strong acid without "drinking" it; that is, without reacting with it and using it up. In 1814, therefore, the Swedish chemist Berzelius decided that this was like Tantalus standing in water but not drinking. He named the element "tantalum" and that is now its name.

Niobe (nie'o-bee) was the daughter of Tantalus, but she did not learn humility from his fate. She had fourteen children, seven sons and seven daughters, and was so proud of their good looks and accomplishments that she felt no other mother could be as lucky. Even Leto, she boasted, only had one daughter and one son.

Of course these children were Apollo and Artemis and, on hearing their mother sneered at, they took revenge. Apollo killed the seven sons with his arrows and Artemis killed the seven daughters with hers.

Niobe, in whose arms the last daughter died, wept ceaselessly for her lost children and eventually, out of pity, the gods turned her into a stone out of which a spring of water continued to run.

Niobe, like her father, Tantalus, also entered the list of chemical elements. In 1801, an English chemist, Charles Hatchett, thought he had located a new element in a rock that had first been found in Connecticut. He named the new element "columbium" after Columbia, a poetic name for the United States.

However, some argument arose as to whether columbium wasn't actually identical with tantalum, which was discovered at about the same time. It wasn't until 1846 that a German chemist, Heinrich Rose, showed that columbium was similar to tantalum but not identical. For the sake of its similarity, however, he suggested that it be named after a close relative of Tantalus; to wit, after his daughter, Niobe. For a long time, American chemists called the element columbium, while the European chemists called it "niobium." A few years ago, the American chemists gave in. The official name everywhere is now niobium.

The moral of "beware hubris" was not the only one the Greeks could draw. There is a well-known myth which has a moral of an entirely different sort. This involves Midas, the son of Gordius. Gordius was the first king of Phrygia (a kingdom in Asia Minor).

Gordius was greeted as king when he rode into the capital city in an ox-cart. It seems an oracle had advised the citizens to accept the next man to enter the city on such a vehicle.

Gordius's first act was to tie the yoke of the ox-cart with the reins in a very complicated knot, to show that he would never have to use that ox-cart again. He announced that anyone who untied that knot would conquer all Asia, and then went on to be king in the city, now renamed "Gordium." Though many tried to untie the knot, none ever succeeded. From that, we still have our phrase "a Gordian knot" to represent a very tangled and insoluble problem.

The legend was mythical but the knot actually existed. At least when Alexander the Great passed through Phrygia in 333 B.C. he was shown the Gordian knot. He made no attempt to untie it. Instead, he drew his sword and calmly cut through it, then went on to conquer all those parts of Asia he could reach with his armies, without once being defeated. From this comes the phrase "to cut the Gordian knot," meaning to solve a complicated problem by direct and unexpected action.

But it was *Midas,* the son of Gordius, whose actions pointed a particular moral. He grew quite wealthy but had his mind entirely fixed on the desire to grow still more wealthy. Because of a favor Midas had done for Dionysus, that god offered Midas a free wish for anything he wanted. At once Midas wished that everything he touched should turn to gold.

We still speak of this as the "Midas touch" or the

"golden touch" and use it to refer to anyone who is particularly successful in business. Everything he touches, so to speak, turns to gold.

However, although most people still admire and envy this ability, the Greeks pointed out the opposite moral. Midas found that his entire palace and all its furnishings turned to gold, as he touched object after object, but that made everything rather monotonous and ugly. Everything he tried to eat and drink turned to gold as soon as he touched it so that he was threatened with starvation. Finally (in a late version of the myth) his daughter ran to him, and turned to gold when he embraced her.

He had to beg Dionysus to withdraw the gift, and Dionysus did. Apparently the moral is one well known to us, whether we believe it or not. It is that "money isn't everything."

The Greeks would not have been human if they weren't interested in romance. It is natural, therefore, that many of their myths should have been what we would call today "love stories." Some of them are very touching and have remained famous for nearly three thousand years.

There is, for instance, the story of *Orpheus* (or'-fyoos), the son of Apollo and Calliope, chief of the Muses. With such parents, it is not surprising that Orpheus should be a sweet singer. At his singing, the very rocks would move closer while wild beasts would lie down tamely to hear.

So famous was he in this respect that "Orphean" still means melodiously enchanting. Similarly, various music halls were called "Orpheum" in his honor, and the name passed on to vaudeville theaters and movie houses.

Orpheus married *Eurydice* (yoo-rid'i-see), but after a short period of happiness, Eurydice was bitten by a snake and died. Orpheus was inconsolable and decided to go down to Hades and get her back. Playing his lyre and singing, he went down to the underworld. So enchanted by his playing was Charon that he took him across; and Cerberus bowed his heads and let Orpheus pass. The shades flocked around, remembering sadly their past lives at the sound of the music, and the tortures in Tartarus stopped while the demons paused to listen.

Tears came even to the iron face of Hades at the approach of Orpheus and he gave the sweet singer back his Eurydice, on one condition: that he never look back to see her until he reached the world above.

Back upward traveled Orpheus, still playing his lyre, still singing. And when he was almost out of Hades, when the light of the sun could already be dimly seen, he could bear it no longer. He turned to see if Eurydice was really following. She was, but when he turned, she suddenly drifted away with a sad cry, holding out her arms helplessly.

Orpheus rushed back downward but now no one would listen. Charon barred him from the boat. Cerberus on the other side growled terribly, and Hades, in the distance, shook his head stonily.

Eurydice was lost!

Orpheus was later made the center of a mystery religion. He had after all been in the underworld and returned. His was one of the most famous mysteries, in fact, and "Orphic" still means "mystical."

Another story is that of a mountain nymph, called *Echo* (from a Greek word meaning "sound"). She had offended Hera with her chattering tongue and had been condemned to almost complete silence. She could only repeat the last words anyone said to her.

Echo fell in love with a handsome young man named *Narcissus,* but she could not make her feelings plain because she could only repeat his last words. Narcissus treated her with unfeeling harshness and scorned her. This was a kind of hubris, and nemesis followed. Narcissus saw his own reflection in the water. He had never seen it before and did not know it was himself he saw. He fell in love with the reflection.

Naturally, that did him no good and it was his turn to be rejected. He pined away and died, turning into a flower which is still called the "narcissus" in his honor. And we still call anyone who is extremely conceited "narcissistic."

As for Echo she pined away, too, until nothing was left of her but her voice, which is still to be heard in the mountains of which she was nymph. Her voice is still called an "echo."

Then there was the case of *Alcyone* (al-sie'-o-nee), a woman happily married to *Ceyx* (see'iks). Unfortunately, Ceyx died in a shipwreck and Alcyone, wild with grief, threw herself into the sea when she heard the news.

The gods, in pity, turned her and her dead husband into kingfishers so that their happiness might continue, even if not in human form. The kingfisher is still called "halcyon" in poetry. (The reason for the initial "h" is that Greek words sometimes started with a sound that doesn't occur in Latin or in English. It somewhat resembles an "h" sound, and words that start with it, as Alcyone does, may be spelled without an initial "h" or with one, in English, depending on taste. For instance, the kingfishers are referred to by zoologists as the "Alcyonidae" (without the initial "h").

Actually, the halcyon of the Greeks is not a real kingfisher but an imaginary bird who the Greeks believed made her nest on the sea and hatched out her chicks there. This was supposed to be done during the two weeks following December 15. At this time, the gods were supposed to keep the ocean dead calm for the sake of the chicks. For this reason, any time of great peace and security is referred to as "halcyon days."

(One last word; the brightest of the Pleiades is called "Alcyone" but this honors a different Alcyone, and not the wife of Ceyx.)

It would seem that the Greek love stories run to tragedy and so they do. Love stories generally do, for sad stories seem to move people more than happy ones do.

Still, love stories with a "happy ending" are to be found among the myths. I'll mention only one, the most famous one, even though it is not really Greek, but was invented by a Roman named Lucius Apuleius about A.D. 150. It is the story of Cupid and *Psyche* (sie'kee).

Psyche was a princess so beautiful that all men fell in love with her. She was considered even more beautiful than Venus. Venus, growing jealous, sent her son Cupid to use his arrows of love to cause her to fall in love with a beggar and thus punish her; nemesis for hubris, in the usual way. (Notice that it is Venus and Cupid here, not Aphrodite and Eros, for the story is Roman, not Greek.)

Cupid is, in this story, pictured as a young man, instead of the usual child. He flew down on his task and as he was about to shoot Psyche, he accidentally wounded himself on one of his own arrows and fell in love with her himself.

He wooed her at night and married her, but never allowed her to see him (for he didn't want the news to get back to Venus). He even forbade her to make any attempt to see him. Psyche's sisters, jealous of this romantic affair, teased Psyche and told her that her husband was really an ugly monster and that was why she was not allowed to see him. Psyche was sufficiently worried about this to bring a lamp secretly to the bed where Cupid was sleeping. She leaned over to look at him and oil from the lamp dropped on his face and woke him. Sorrowfully, he left her.

The rest of the story concerns the manner in which Psyche wanders through the world, and even down into Hades, going through great troubles and hardships imposed on her by the angry Venus; but searching, always searching, for her Cupid. Eventually, her faithfulness won her the forgiveness of Venus. Psyche was made immortal and joined Cupid forever in heaven.

Now this is more than just a love story. Psyche is the Greek word for "soul" and behind the actual events of the story lay a deeper meaning. (A story with a deeper meaning hidden behind the surface meaning is an "allegory.") The soul (Psyche), originally in heaven where all is love (Cupid), is condemned for a period to wander through the earth, undergoing misery and hardship. Still, if it is faithful and true, the story points out, it will eventually return to heaven and be reunited with love.

The situation is like that of the ugly caterpillar which, after a while, seems to die and be buried in a cocoon like a man in a tomb. But then it breaks out as a beautiful butterfly, just as a man's soul breaks out into a better life. It is with this thought in mind that artists usually picture Psyche with the wings of a butterfly. (The popularity of the Psyche story later led to having fairies drawn in the same way.) There is even a group of moths with the family name of "Psychidae," showing that zoologists are acquainted with the myth, too.

The word "psyche" in its meaning of mind or soul is also part of our language. "Psychology" is the study of the mind and a "psychiatrist" is a doctor who specializes in mental disorders. A person who is supposed to sense things with his mind, rather than with his eyes, ears, or other ordinary senses, is said to be "psychic."

Psyche lives in the heavens literally, too, for the sixteenth asteroid to be discovered was named "Psyche."

Occasionally a myth proves to be not entirely fiction. Instead, it represents a memory of great days in the past. In the times before writing was widespread and before history was written, the only way past events were remembered was by word of mouth. A father would tell his son who would tell his son and so on.

Then some minstrel would make up a song about it and would improve matters to make them dramatic. Each following minstrel would add his own improvements. In the end, there would be a myth or legend that would be full of all sorts of fantastic things, but at the core would still be the historical event.

For instance, in the Greek myths, the island of Crete had considerable importance. Zeus, as a baby, was brought up on Crete, and when he kidnaped Europa, he brought her to Crete. There the son of Europa, named *Minos,* became king of a rich and powerful nation.

So important and just were he and his brother, *Rhadamanthus* (rad'a-man'thus) that Zeus placed them in Hades after death to serve as judges of the dead. "Rhadamanthine" is a word sometimes used, therefore, to mean "rigorously just."

The Greek myths described Crete under Minos as having a hundred large cities, as having a navy that ruled all the islands, as having conquered parts of Greece itself, as worshiping bulls and so on.

This was taken with a grain of salt by later historians. In the great days of Greece, Crete hardly counted. It was a backward land without much civilization of importance. It produced nothing but pirates and brigands. Surely, such a hillbilly region couldn't ever have been great and powerful.

Then in the 1890's, the English archeologist Arthur John Evans began to dig into old ruins in Crete. To the amazement of the world, he found signs of a high civilization in Crete that dated back many centuries before the great days of Greece.

The ancient Cretans did have gorgeous palaces and cities; better ones, in fact, than the Greeks ever had. They even had internal plumbing, which the Greeks never had. They had a great navy, and did control the islands about Greece and even Greece itself. They left artwork showing their religious ceremonies and bulls did indeed play a great part.

The myths about Minos, in other words, represented memories of an actual great civilization and had a core of history. In fact, there are some people who think that the Greek story about Atlantis might refer to Crete, too. Plato and the other Greeks of the time couldn't really believe that the great land of myth could exist in the backward island of Crete, so they set Atlantis in the western Ocean where all wonderful things were.

Evans acknowledged the value of the myths by referring to this ancient civilization as "Minoan," and that is what it has been called ever since.

One of the most famous tales told in the myths about Minos and his kingdom involves the Athenian *Daedalus* (ded'uh-lus). Daedalus was a kind of mythical Edison, who worked out all sorts of ingenious inventions. As examples, he is supposed to have invented the saw, the ax and the gimlet. For this reason, the word "daedalian" means skillful or inventive.

Daedalus traveled to Crete and while there built a large maze for Minos. No one entering that maze could ever find his way out again. This was called the *Labyrinth* and the word still exists in our time to mean such a maze and anything else that contains complicated, winding passages.

For instance, the inner ear has such a complicated form that it is sometimes called the "membranous labyrinth." Part of the kidney, containing very complicated little tubes, is also called the "labyrinth." Certain extinct ancestors of modern frogs had teeth containing very complex patterns of bone. Those belong to a group now called the

"Labyrinthodonta" ("labyrinth teeth"). Certain modern fishes have gill regions that are very complex in form and these belong to the group "Labyrinthibranchii ("labyrinth gills").

Building the labyrinth did Daedalus no good, however, for he quarreled with Minos and Minos had him and his son *Icarus* (ik'uh-rus), imprisoned. Daedalus, fearing execution, wanted very much to escape from Crete, but Minos' ships controlled the seas all about the island. To get away from the island of Crete without being captured by the navy, Daedalus would have to escape by air.

Consequently, the clever Daedalus built wings out of bird's feathers which he attached to a light frame by means of wax. He made a pair for himself and another for Icarus. Attaching them to their arms, they rose into the air and flew away.

Daedalus had warned Icarus not to fly too high but Icarus, overcome with the joy of flying and the feeling of power it gave him, could not resist the impulse to show this power by flying higher and higher. (That was hubris.) In doing this, Icarus met nemesis at once, for he flew too near the sun. Its heat melted the wax that held the feathers, the wings fell apart, and Icarus tumbled into a section of the sea just off the southwest coast of modern Turkey. This is still called the "Icarian Sea."

As for Daedalus, he escaped safely, but sorrowing, to Sicily.

The memory of this first air casualty leaves its traces in the name of a very unusual planetoid discovered in 1948 by the American astronomer Walter Baade. This planetoid travels a path which at some points is farther from the sun than is the orbit of Mars. Then, like Icarus, the planetoid starts swooping toward the sun and approaches as close as 17 million miles. This is closer to the sun than Mercury ever gets. It is closer than any known object (except for an occasional comet) ever gets to the sun.

And so the planetoid has been named Icarus.

Other myths also concerned themselves with the explanation of how certain pieces of knowledge arose. For instance, a man named *Boötes* (buh-o'teez), which in

Greek means "herdsman," is supposed to have invented the plow. He was set in the heavens as a reward and the constellation of "Boötes" is to be found there. It contains the bright star Arcturus, which I mentioned earlier in the book.

Again, there is the case of *Cadmus*, a brother of the girl, Europa, whom Zeus had carried off. Cadmus left Phoenicia, where he and Europa had lived, and traveled to Greece in search of her. He is supposed to have invented the alphabet, which was therefore sometimes called the "Cadmean letters."

Here again is a case of accurate history in the myths. The alphabet was invented by Phoenicians in actual fact. The Greeks did indeed get their alphabet from Phoenicians.

After fruitless wandering, Cadmus settled in the territory of Boeotia and founded the Greek city of Thebes. There, on the advice of the gods, he planted the teeth of a dragon he had killed. They sprouted into armed men in a matter of minutes. They would have killed Cadmus, but he threw a stone at them. It struck one, who, imagining the blow came from a neighbor, lashed out. At once there was a battle royal and all but five were soon dead. The surviving five then served Cadmus faithfully and became the ancestors of the Thebans.

As a result of this story, the phrase "to sow dragon's teeth" means to stir up war or other troubles. A "Cadmean victory" is one in which hardly anyone survives. (There is a chemical element named "cadmium" which was isolated from an ore that was called "cadmia" by the ancients, perhaps because it was first found near the Cadmean city of Thebes.

IN THE EARLY DAYS, according to the myths, gods and men associated freely. Children were born with one parent a god and one human. Such children were demigods occasionally. Sometimes they were merely human, but of unusual strength and bravery. These were *heroes*.

The age in which the heroes lived was called the "Heroic Age." As a result, any period in a nation's history when there were many stirring events and many brave men is now termed a "Heroic Age."

The Greeks made up innumerable legends about these supermen, these offspring of man and god. Each succeeding mythmaker made the heroes he sang of even more heroic than the mythmaker before had done. The result was that the hero legends became rousing adventure stories with strong elements of fantasy. (Now, however, the word has come to mean any brave man; or just the main character of a story, even if he is not particularly brave.)

One such legend, for instance, involved the hero *Perseus* (per'syoos), who was pictured as the son of Zeus. He and his mother, *Danae* (day'nuh-ee), were refugees at the court of a king who intended to force an unwelcome marriage on Danae. To save his mother Perseus offered to ransom her by bringing back the head of the dreadful Gorgon, Medusa.

Since Perseus was a son of Zeus and was loved by the gods, they helped him. Athena gave him a polished shield so that he could see Medusa by reflection only and avoid being turned to stone. Hermes gave him a magic sword and Hades gave him a helmet which would make him invisible when worn. Perseus also collected flying sandals and a special bag in which to hold Medusa's head. These were obtained from certain nymphs whom he only reached after various adventures.

Perseus found the Gorgons sleeping, swooped down on his flying sandals, invisible thanks to his helmet. He used Athena's polished shield to see with, aimed Hermes' sword at Medusa, cut her head off and put it in the bag. Medusa's sisters woke and pursued him, shrieking horribly, but he flew swiftly and escaped.

On his way back, Perseus passed Atlas, whom he showed Medusa's head out of pity. Atlas was turned into a huge stone mountain and his punishment was ended.

Perseus also passed a southern kingdom where another drama was taking place. The king of the land was *Cepheus* (see'fyoos) and the queen was *Cassiopeia* (cas'ee-oh-pee'uh). They had a beautiful daughter named *Andromeda* (an-drom'i-duh) and Cassiopeia was so vain that she boasted that she and her daughter were more beautiful than the Nereids, the nymphs of the sea. This was hubris, and nemesis followed quickly.

Poseidon, to avenge the honor of the Nereids, sent a sea monster to ravage the coasts of the land. The only way to make it leave, said the oracles, was to sacrifice Andromeda to it. So Andromeda was chained to a rock at the shore, while father and mother stood weeping by.

Perseus flew by just as the sea-monster was approaching Andromeda. Diving rapidly, he took Medusa's head out of its bag and showed it to the monster, who turned to stone. Perseus married Andromeda and took her back with him to where his mother still waited. He had Medusa's head with him, but when he said so, the king and courtiers laughed at him and denied his story as a boastful tale. As proof, he took the head out of the bag and turned them all to stone.

Perseus then gave Medusa's head to Athena, who placed it in the middle of her shield, making it a perfect protection. Not only did it ward off spears and swords but anyone approaching was turned to stone before an attack could even be made. Athena's shield (which she originally got from Zeus) was called *Aegis* (ee'jis) and that word, sometimes spelled "egis," is still used in the language to refer to any strong protection or defense.

The story of Perseus was very popular with the Greeks and they filled the sky with constellations representing the various characters in it. "Perseus" is the name given to a constellation near Taurus.

The most remarkable star in the constellation is one sometimes called the "Demon star." It is the second brightest star in the constellation and is therefore also called "Beta Persei" ("beta" being the second letter of the Greek alphabet).

Every two and a half days, Algol suddenly loses most of its brightness over a period of five hours and then regains it in five more hours. We now know that this is because Algol has a dimmer companion which circles it and occasionally gets in the way of its light, eclipsing it. To the Greeks, however, who knew nothing about this, the loss of light seemed remarkable and against nature, since almost none of the other stars seemed to behave so. It must have seemed fitting then to make such a monstrous star represent Medusa. Perhaps that star was the cause of their placing Perseus in that particular collection of stars.

In August, there is often a display of meteors as the earth passes through a section of space in which a large collection of these small pebbles follow a path around the sun. The meteors seem to come out of a portion of the sky in the constellation Perseus, and so they are called the "Perseids."

Right next to the constellation Perseus is the constellation Andromeda. And to the north are the constellations of Cassiopeia and Cepheus.

The constellation Cepheus contains only dim stars. It seemed right that in the skies, as in the myth, the king should be outshone by his strong-minded queen, for Cassiopeia contains five bright stars. However, the Greeks could not have foretold that one of the stars in Cepheus was to make him unexpectedly famous.

The star in the right leg of Cepheus is called "Delta Cephei" ("delta" is the fourth letter in the Greek alphabet). Delta Cephei, like Algol, changes its brightness. However, Algol is eclipsed, but not so Delta Cephei. Delta Cephei, astronomers found out, pulsates. It gets larger and smaller in a regular motion. Afterward, astronomers found that a number of stars pulsated in this manner, growing dimmer and brighter. In honor of the first such star to be discovered, the whole class of pulsating stars was called "Cepheids."

In 1912 an American astronomer, Henrietta Leavitt, discovered how to use the Cepheids to find the distance of far-off objects in space where no other method could be used. As a result, Cepheids have become extremely important in astronomy and are very closely studied. It is amusing to think that objects so important in astronomy are called by a word that traces back to an obscure and henpecked mythical king.

Even the sea monster that was to devour Andromeda is to be found in the sky. It is there as the constellation *Cetus* (which can be translated as "whale" or "sea monster").

One other portion of the Perseus myth remains to be told. When Perseus cut off Medusa's head, drops of blood fell to the ground and out of them was formed, full grown, a beautiful winged horse called *Pegasus* (peg'uh-sus).

Any fiery and swift horse can be called a "pegasus." To any lover of horses, it would seem a shame that something like Pegasus never really existed. To be sure, there is a small fish with large fins sticking out of either side of the body like a pair of wings, and that is nowadays called

"Pegasus" by zoologists. However, it is certainly a poor substitute for the beautiful horse.

Pegasus was used by another hero, *Bellerophon* (bel-er'o-fon), as a mount. Riding on Pegasus, he slew the horrible Chimaera. (Ever since, knights on horses have been slaying dragons in the fairy tales.)

Right next to the constellation Andromeda is that of Pegasus. The three brightest stars in this constellation, together with the brightest star in Andromeda, form a large square which is called the "Square of Pegasus."

Sometimes the Greeks managed to get their heroes into a large group, a kind of "myth-spectacular" for increased excitement. An example was the hunting of the "Calydonian boar."

The chief hero involved here was *Meleager* (mel'ee-ay'jer) the son of the king of Calydon in central Greece. When Meleager was born, the Fates told his mother, *Althaea* (al-thee'uh), that the baby would live only until a certain burning piece of wood in the fire (a "brand") was completely burned. Althaea at once seized the brand, put out the flame and hid it.

When Meleager grew to manhood, Artemis, who was offended at the king of Calydon, sent a large boar to ravage the lands. Meleager organized a hunting expedition to trap and kill the boar and many heroes came to join the party.

Among them, for instance, were *Castor* and *Polydeuces* (pol'ee-dyoo'seez). These were twin brothers, but while Polydeuces was immortal, Castor was not. These twins were called the *Dioscuri* (die'-os-kyoo'ree), which means the "sons of god" or, really, "sons of Zeus." They were greatly honored later by the Romans, who called Polydeuces *Pollux*. It is as Castor and Pollux that the twins are best known to us.

Their birth, in fact, involves a famous myth. Zeus wooed *Leda,* their mother, by turning himself into a swan. Eventually, Leda gave birth to two eggs. In one was Polydeuces and a girl, *Helen*. In the other was Castor and another girl, *Clytemnestra* (klie'tem-nes'truh). Both girls were important in myths I shall mention later.

Zeus, as usual, honored the animal form he had taken by placing it among the constellations. That constellation is now known as *Cygnus* (sig'nus), which in Latin means "swan."

Castor and Polydeuces carried on a great feud with another pair of twins, *Idas* (eye'dus) and *Lynceus* (lin'-syoos), who were also present at the boar hunt. Of these two, Idas was the better fighter, but Lynceus was renowned for his sharp eyesight, being able to see through rocks. Cats, of course, are supposed to have sharp eyes, and one variety of large cat is still called "lynx," though, of course, it can no more see through rocks than any other creature can. People with very good eyesight are still said to be "lynx-eyed."

The climax of the feud came when, in a battle royal, Lynceus was killed by Castor who was killed by Idas who was killed by Polydeuces. Polydeuces, being immortal, could not die, but such was his love for his brother that he prayed to Zeus to take away his immortality unless he could share it with Castor. As a result, Zeus let both spend their days alternately in heaven and in Hades.

Castor and Polydeuces are to be found among the constellations. The third sign of the zodiac is *Gemini* (jem'i-nee) which, in Latin, means "twins." The constellation contains two bright stars, one called "Castor" and one "Pollux." Pollux is somewhat the brighter of the two, as is reasonable since Pollux (Polydeuces) was the immortal brother. Probably the existence of two bright stars so close to each other was what gave the Greeks the notion of making it a twin constellation. A trace of the old Roman respect for the twins remains. We still swear by them when we say "By Jiminy."

Another hero present at the hunting of the Calydonian boar was *Theseus* (thee'syoos) the Athenian. He was the pet of the Athenian mythmakers and his most famous adventure is one in which he freed Athens of the necessity of paying tribute to King Minos.

Every year Athens had to send seven young men and seven young women to Crete, where Minos fed them to a monster with a man's body and a bull's head. The monster was the *Minotaur* (min'oh-tawr) or "bull of Minos" and it was kept in the Labyrinth. In fact, it was to keep the Minotaur that Daedalus built the Labyrinth.

The agreement was that if ever the Athenians could kill the Minotaur and then get out of the Labyrinth, the tribute would be ended.

When the time of tribute came one year, Theseus, who was the son of *Aegeus* (ee'jee-us), king of Athens, and who was now grown to manhood, had himself included as one of the young men. In Crete, *Ariadne* (a'ree-ad'nee), daughter of Minos, fell in love with Theseus and gave him a ball of twine which he could use to find his way out of the Labyrinth. Theseus entered with the others, unwound the ball of twine as he walked, met and killed the Minotaur, then followed the twine out of the Labyrinth. The tribute was ended.

On previous occasions, the Athenian ship which carried the young people to Crete used black sails, going and returning, out of mourning. Theseus had promised Aegeus that he would defeat the Minotaur and would return with white sails signifying joy. However, Theseus forgot to change the sails, in all the excitement.

Aegeus, watching for the ship from a high rock, saw the black sails, assumed Theseus was dead and in despair plunged into the sea to his death. As a result the portion of the Mediterranean sea between Greece and Turkey is called the "Aegean Sea."

Theseus, in his time, was supposed to have wandered over the Athenian portion of Greece, destroying monsters and killing brigands (like the heroes on our modern television Westerns). One of his most famous encounters was with a robber called *Procrustes* (pro-crus'teez). Procrustes had a bed in which he forced his victims to lie. If they were too long for the bed, he cut off portions of their legs. If they were too short he pulled their legs out of joint to stretch them. Either way they were made to fit the bed.

Theseus killed him. Ever since, however, any attempt to force people into a particular way of thinking or behaving has been termed "procrustean."

Another famous adventure of Theseus involved an expedition against the *Amazons,* a group of warrior women supposed to live in Asia Minor. Many of the Greek heroes fought against them. Usually the heroes won. Theseus did, too. He carried away the queen of the Amazons, who was named *Hippolyta* (hi-pol'i-tuh) and married her. (Shakespeare's play, *A Midsummer Night's Dream,* is supposed to take place in Athens during the holiday period that preceded the marriage of Theseus and Hippolyta.)

Strong, muscular women, especially those who do a man's work, have been called "amazons" ever since. In 1541, a Spanish explorer named Francisco de Orellana, was sailing up a large South American river, which had been discovered forty years earlier and which had been called by various names. At one point he had to fight a battle with natives and it seemed to him that the women of the tribe were fighting along with the men. For this reason, he named the river the "Amazon River" and it has kept that name ever since.

However, to return to the Calydonian boar hunt, the most remarkable member was *Atalanta,* a kind of Amazon herself, for she was a woman who specialized in hunting and could outdo most men in athletic contests.

Meleager fell in love with her but his two uncles (the brothers of Meleager's mother, Althaea) disliked her, being superstitious about allowing a woman to engage in a man's occupation.

The hunt was long and hard, but Atalanta was the first to wound the boar, and Meleager himself finally killed it. Meleager skinned the boar and offered the skin as a gesture of honor to Atalanta for drawing first blood.

Meleager's uncles objected violently to this and Meleager, growing angry, drew his sword and killed them both. When this news was carried to Althaea, she was overcome with a spasm of grief for her brothers. Angrily, she snatched the unburned brand she had saved ever since Meleager's babyhood and threw it in the fire where it burned. As it did, Meleager was overcome with sudden weakness and died.

Because of this, any object on which a man's life or reputation depends and by which he can be destroyed, is called an "Althaea's brand."

At the news of Meleager's death, his sisters wailed and shrieked continuously and were changed by the gods into guinea hens, which have continued their wild shrieking ever since. In fact, "meleagris" is the Latin word for "guinea fowl" and it is still used today as a zoological name for the creatures.

Another gathering of heroes took place on the occasion of the expedition to get the "Golden Fleece." The Golden Fleece was kept in the land of Colchis (kol'kis) which was located at the eastern tip of the Black Sea, near the Caucasus Mountains.

Now the Caucasus Mountains were just about the eastern end of the world to the Greeks of the mythmaking age. It was as far east as they could go without leaving the Mediterranean. They heard some rumors of the Caspian Sea, which lay to the east of the Caucasus, and were under the impression that the Caspian was just an inlet of the ocean-river that encircled the earth.

The Greeks put almost as many wonders into this far east, as they put into the far west. Prometheus was chained to the Caucasus; and Helios was supposed to begin his westward journey at Colchis (just a way of saying that Colchis was the most easterly city in the world).

Just north of the Black Sea, the Greeks imagined a land inhabited by people called *Cimmerians* (si-mee'ree-anz). These were supposed to live in eternal darkness (the result, perhaps, of vague rumors the Greeks heard of the Arctic region where the sun actually doesn't shine for days or even months at a time). From this comes the phrase "Cimmerian darkness" for darkness that is deep indeed. The peninsula of Crimea, on the north shore of the Black Sea and now a part of the Soviet Union, is a version of the word Cimmeria.

In any case, among the other wonders, the *Golden Fleece* existed at Colchis. It was supposed to be the pelt of a flying ram sent down by Zeus to save the lives of a young man named *Phrixus* and his sister, *Helle*, who were in danger of being killed by a wicked stepmother. The two youngsters climbed upon the ram's back and it flew (in magic fashion) swiftly toward Colchis.

When passing over the first set of narrow straits that

separate Europe and Asia, Helle fell off and drowned. That strait was therefore called "Hellespont" ("sea of Helle"). In modern times the name has been changed, as I shall mention later. However, the tip of the Gallipolli Peninsula, on the European side of the strait, is still called "Cape Helle."

At Colchis, the ram was sacrificed to Zeus and its golden fleece was hung in a temple where it was guarded by an unsleeping dragon. The ram was also placed in the zodiac as the constellation *Aries* (ay'ruh-eez), which is the Latin word for "ram." In ancient times, the sun entered Aries at the time of the spring equinox and that made Aries the first sign of the zodiac. It still is considered this, even though the spring equinox (which shifts position slowly from year to year) is no longer in Aries but is now in Pisces.

The plot of the story next turns to *Jason* whose father, *Aeson* (ee'son), had been king of the city of Iolcus (eye-ol'kus) in northern Greece. *Pelias,* the brother of Aeson, had taken over the throne by force and Aeson with his son, Jason, had fled. Once grown to manhood, Jason returned to Iolcus and claimed the throne. Pelias, to get rid of him, offered him the throne in exchange for the Golden Fleece, expecting Jason to die in the attempt to get it.

Jason accepted the challenge and sent out a call to all the heroes to gather and aid him. Forty-nine of them did (with Jason making a total of fifty) and a ship was built with fifty oars. The Greeks supposed this to be the first large ship ever built. It was called the *Argo* after the designer of the ship, *Argus.* (However, the Greek word "argos" means "swift" and that could have been the reason for the naming of the ship.) The fifty heroes who sailed for the Golden Fleece are therefore called the *Argonauts* ("sailors of the Argo").

(Oddly enough, the word "argosy" meaning a large ship with a rich cargo has no connection with the *Argo*. The word "argosy" is a twisted version of the seaport named "Ragusa" from which such ships would set sail in ancient times.)

The *Argo* was such a famous ship that it was placed

among the constellations. It is located far to the south and only parts of it can be seen from the latitude of Greece. It is a large constellation, and would be the largest in the sky except that it is now broken up into four smaller constellations. These are *Vela* (vee'luh), which means "sail" in Latin, *Carina* (kuh-ree'nuh), which means "keel," *Puppis* (pup'is), which means "stern," and *Pyxis* (pik'sis), which means "compass."

As for the word "Argonaut," that leaves a trace in zoology. There is a certain sea creature, a relative of the octopus, the female of which forms a delicate and beautiful shell. The ancients supposed the creature used the shell as a sail and so the creature was called "nautilus" which, in Greek, means "sailor."

In modern times, it was named the "paper nautilus," because of the delicacy of the shell and to distinguish it from other creatures also called "nautilus." Linnaeus, the great classifier of plants and animals, put the paper nautilus in the order "Argonauta." The scientific name of the paper nautilus is "Argonauta argo." However, since it does not use the shell as a sail, the creature is not really a sailor despite its name.

Some of the heroes of the Calydonian boar hunt were also present among the Argonauts. Castor, Polydeuces, Idas, Lynceus, Atalanta, and Meleager were among the group. (How the last two could be there when Meleager supposedly met Atalanta at the hunt and died shortly after is not explained, but then one mythmaker doesn't worry about the next, sometimes.) Present also was Orpheus, who had not yet married Eurydice.

The Argonauts traveled across the Aegean Sea, landing on islands where they feasted with friendly inhabitants or battled suspicious ones. At one point they drove off the Harpies who were carrying on a campaign of annoyance against a blind king.

To enter the Black Sea, they had to pass between two moving rocks called the *Symplegades* (sim-pleg'-uh-deez), which comes from Greek words meaning "striking together." These clashed together forcefully every once in a while and ships trying to pass through were crushed. The Argonauts let loose a dove which flew between the

rocks. They clashed and, as they moved back, the Argonauts drove the *Argo* through at top speed. Before the
rocks could come together again, the *Argo* had passed
safely and the Symplegades were fixed, never to move
again.

Eventually, after a battle with birds which dropped
metal feathers like spears, they reached Colchis.

The daughter of the king of Colchis was *Medea* (me-
dee'uh), who fell in love with Jason, just as Ariadne had
fallen in love with Theseus. Medea helped him kill the
dragon (a child of Echidna) that guarded the Fleece by
giving him a special lotion that protected him against its
breath of fire.

Once they had the Golden Fleece, Medea helped Jason
escape with it, using spells and stratagems to fight off the
pursuing ships. Only once were they in real danger and
that was when they passed the Sirens. Here, however,
Orpheus came to the rescue. He outsang them. All ears
were for Orpheus and the Sirens went unheard.

Back in Iolcus, Jason married Medea and regained his
throne.

Medea, to the Greeks, was the prize example of a
female magician, or witch. They kept making up horrible
stories about her. However, what seems basic is that she
knew the healing properties of various herbs. For instance, there is one passage in the myth which tells how
she restored youth to Jason's old father by having him
drink a special potion.

Now before the days of modern medicine, women who
could use herbs to cure disease were looked upon with
fear. Might they not use their knowledge to poison as well
as cure if they were crossed? Even in quite modern times,
women who were too acquainted with plant remedies were
in trouble over it.

And yet, it is just barely possible that Medea's treat-
ments may have left one important trace. Our word "medicine" may trace back to her. It is only a suggestion, for
no one is quite sure how this word actually arose, but that
it arose from Medea is an interesting theory, and I rather
like it.

The greatest of the Greek heroes was *Heracles* (her'uh-kleez), who is better known by the Latin version of his name, *Hercules* (her'kyoo-leez). Heracles was a tall, strong, muscular man, always pictured as dressed in a lion's skin and carrying a gigantic club.

He had superhuman strength and accomplished superhuman tasks. The Greeks delighted in making up more and more stories about him. Eventually, scarcely a myth could be told without dragging in Heracles somehow, until a proverb arose, "Nothing without Heracles."

He was a kind of Paul Bunyan of the ancient world, so that the word "herculean" means something either of superhuman difficulty or of superhuman strength. It would be impossible to run through all the myths about Heracles in this book, even briefly, so I will just mention those that have left traces in the language.

To begin with, Heracles is honored among the stars by the constellation "Hercules." It contains a globular cluster of stars which is the brightest to be seen in the northern hemisphere. In 1934, a star in this cluster exploded and grew so bright it could be seen with the naked eye. Such an exploding star is called a "nova." This particular one, the brightest in recent years, was called "Nova Herculis."

Heracles was a son of Zeus and a mortal woman, *Alcmena* (alk-mee'nuh). Of course, Hera was jealous. Through trickery, she got Zeus to swear that the next child born in the royal house of the city of Thebes was to be king. Zeus did so, knowing that Heracles was about to be born. Hera then delayed Heracles' birth just long enough for another prince of the same house, *Eurystheus* (yoo-ris'thyoos), to be born first. In this way, Heracles was condemned to serve Eurystheus until he had achieved twelve great tasks.

Another explanation is that Heracles went mad as he did every once in a while in the myths. When he was mad, he could not control his own strength but killed everyone in sight. As atonement for such killings, he undertook the twelve labors.

Still a third explanation is a highly moral one made up considerably later than the others. Heracles was supposed to have been approached by "Pleasure" and "Virtue."

Pleasure offered him a life of ease and delight. Virtue offered him a life of toil, with immortality at the end. Heracles chose the latter and, after many labors, became a god. To choose the path of virtue over pleasure is still sometimes called "the choice of Heracles."

As for the labors that Heracles underwent, whether out of Hera's spite, or his own madness, or his free choice, the first was to kill the Nemean lion. This was a lion of huge size and strength that was ravaging the district about the city of Nemea. It was supposed to be one of the children of Echidna and its hide was so tough that neither sword nor arrow could penetrate and even Heracles' club broke against it. Eventually, Heracles killed it by strangling it with his bare hands. He stripped off its skin and wore it the rest of his life as the best protection against weapons.

The Nemean lion finds its place in the stars as the fifth sign of the zodiac, *Leo* (the Latin word for "lion"). The constellation contains a bright star in the forepaw of the lion. This is called "Alpha Leonis" by astronomers but "Regulus" is its more familiar name. This means "little King," an appropriate name for a star that is found in the king of beasts.

As his second labor, Heracles destroyed another of the children of Echidna, the Hydra. It lived in a marsh in a district called Lerne and was therefore called the "Lernean Hydra." At first, as Heracles cut the heads off the Hydra (it had nine, you may remember) new heads kept growing back. Heracles therefore had a nephew of his use a burning log to sear each neck as a head was lopped off. In this way new heads could not grow back. The ninth head of the Hydra was immortal and Heracles had to bury it, still snapping away, under a huge rock.

While Heracles was performing this labor, Hera (always jealous) sent a crab to nip at his heels. Heracles crushed it but Hera, in gratitude for the efforts of the creature, set it among the stars. It is now the fourth sign of the zodiac, *Cancer* (the Latin word for "crab," remember). Both Leo and Cancer are on the side of the zodiac opposite the constellation Hercules, as though both feared to tangle with the hero again.

On June 21, when the sun is as far north as it ever gets,

it was in the constellation of Cancer during ancient times. It then shines directly over a line that passes through central Mexico, southern Egypt, India, and southern China. This is called the "Tropic of Cancer," in consequence.

After capturing a deer of superhuman speed and a boar of superhuman strength, taking both alive, Heracles undertook his fifth labor. This was to clean stables that belonged to a king named *Augeias* (aw-jee'us). He was required to do this in one day. Since the stables hadn't been cleaned in thirty years and since three thousand cattle had been kept in it, the accumulation of filth was tremendous. Ever since, anything that is extremely filthy or corrupt has been referred to as an "Augean stable."

Heracles accomplished this task by diverting two rivers which sent their currents through the stables, washing them clean. And so, to end crime or corruption by strong and sudden action is "to cleanse the Augean stables."

Heracles next had to conquer birds with metallic feathers, a fire-breathing bull, man-eating horses and the entire Amazon army. For his tenth labor, though, he had to take a long trip to the far west where the marvels were. He had to fetch cattle that belonged to a monster called *Geryon* (jee'-ree-on) who lived on an island in the western Ocean. Geryon had three heads and six arms and the cattle were further guarded by a two-headed dog named *Orthrus,* another child of Echidna.

Heracles accomplished this, of course. But in passing the western end of the Mediterranean, he split Spain from Africa where, apparently, they had previously been joined together. The two cliffs on either side of the strait were called by the ancients "the pillars of Heracles" for that reason. This phrase is still sometimes used as a poetic synonym for the Strait of Gibraltar (a name which arose only in the Middle Ages).

In the eleventh labor, Heracles had to retrace his steps and go back to the far west to fetch the golden apples of the Hesperides. (The Hesperides, as you may remember, were daughters of Atlas.) These were guarded by a dragon just as the Golden Fleece was.

In one version of the myth, Heracles is supposed to have tricked Atlas into getting them. In another, he himself did the job, slaying the dragon in the process. Hera, always grateful to any enemy of Heracles, put the dragon in the heavens as the constellation *Draco* (dray'ko), which is Latin for "dragon." Draco winds its starry way between Ursa Major and Ursa Minor, and its head lies between those two constellations and the constellation of Hercules.

Heracles who, in the constellation, is pictured with his eternal club, of course, seems to be raising it to kill the dragon once again.

On his way back from the accomplishment of this task, Heracles passed through Africa and, among other adventures, met a race of tiny people, with whom he had a comic interlude, something like that of Gulliver and the Lilliputians.

The Greeks firmly believed that there were tiny people living in Africa somewhere south of Egypt. They called them *Pygmies* from a Greek word meaning "fist." This meant that the people were only as tall as the distance from the elbow to the knuckles of the clenched fist of a normal man. This would make them about fourteen inches high. Naturally, the mythmakers kept making them smaller until they were only as big as a fist, or four inches high.

Ever since, any creature smaller than the usual run of its type has been called "pygmy." Then, when in the nineteenth century, a race of small Negroes was actually found in Africa, these were called Pygmies, though their average height proved to be four and a half feet or so, and not four inches or even fourteen inches.

For his twelfth and last labor, Heracles brought Cerberus up from Hades. In addition to all this, Heracles accompanied the Argonauts part of the way, captured many cities, fought many duels and rescued many damsels in distress.

When his death finally came, it was as tragic as his life had been laborious. Late in life, he married a beautiful woman named *Deianeira* (dee'yuh-nie'-ruh). At one time, while crossing a river in flood, a Centaur named *Nessus* offered to help Deianeira across. He tried to make off with her, however, and Deianeira shrieked to Heracles for help. Instantly, Heracles shot Nessus with his poisoned arrows. (The poison he used had been obtained from the Hydra, and no poison was deadlier or more incurable.)

The dying Nessus, in revenge, told Deianeira to take the garment he wore, which had been soaked in his blood, and keep it. If ever she thought Heracles was losing interest in her, she should give him the garment to wear and his love would be renewed.

Sure enough, some years later, Deianeira suspected that Heracles no longer loved her. She gave him the Centaur's garment and urged Heracles to wear it. Not knowing where it had come from, Heracles put it on, and instantly the Hydra poison penetrated his body.

So fierce was the pain that Heracles felt himself going mad and knew that if this happened, he would kill everyone in sight. He quickly ordered a fire to be built and leaped into it to his death, while Deianeira killed herself in grief.

Ever since, a fatal gift has been termed "a shirt of Nessus."

However, the Greeks provided a happy ending to the story. Heracles was raised to heaven, where Hera finally forgave him. He was married to Hebe, the goddess of youth, and after his long, laborious life, he settled back to the eternity of bliss which he had earned.

8 THE SIEGE OF TROY

THE MOST FAMOUS of all the Greek hero myths were those that concerned a war fought by the Greeks against the city of Troy.

These were made famous for all time by two long poems written about those heroes around 850 B.C. by a legendary poet named *Homer*. These were considered the greatest of all works of literature by the ancient Greeks and we still consider them among the greatest today. The poems of Homer dealt with only a small portion of the Troy myths but other, lesser poets filled in the rest.

So famous is Homer for dealing with great actions that "Homeric" is often used to mean "sublime" or "majestic." However, in one part of the poems Homer describes the gods as laughing without being able to stop at the sight of lame Hephaestus bustling about. For that reason, long fits of uncontrolled laughter, though anything but sublime or majestic, are called "Homeric laughter."

In the Troy myths, the Greek forces were under the king of the city of *Mycenae* (mie-see′nee), which was pictured as the greatest city in Greece, with *Tiryns* (ti'rinz), another important city. Troy was supposed to be in Asia Minor near the Hellespont and to rule the territory about the straits leading from the Mediterranean to the Black Sea.

During most of modern times, historians believed the Trojan War to be a complete legend. Mycenae and Tiryns were but tiny ruined villages and as for Troy, they doubted that any such town ever existed.

In 1868, however, a German businessman named Heinrich Schliemann began to dig at the place where he thought Troy might exist. He loved the poems of Homer and believed they were true, so he was willing to put his own fortune into the digging. To the amazement of the whole world, he found traces of ancient cities on the site of Troy.

Then, in the 1870's, he went to Greece and dug at the sites of Mycenae and Tiryns and discovered the ruins of cities that were far older than the ordinary Greek cities. After Evans went on to discover the ancient civilization of Crete, that settled the matter. There had been a Troy and a Trojan war.

Apparently, what happened was this: The first Greeks entered Greece before 2000 B.C. They came under the influence of the Minoan civilization which was already established in Crete and the islands about Greece. The cities of Mycenae and Tiryns were established.

About 1400 B.C. a new wave of Greeks invaded Greece, these being called the *Achaeans* (uh-kee'-uns). They helped destroy the Cretan rule and took over the Greek world. (The myth of Theseus and the Minotaur may be a memory of this.) Under the Achaeans, Mycenae became the most powerful city in Greece, surrounded by huge "cyclopean" walls. This was called the "Mycenean Age."

The Achaeans reached out for trade with districts in the Black Sea. Greece itself is a mountainous country where agriculture is difficult, but the cities around the Black Sea grew grain in plenty. (The expedition of the Argonauts is a memory of this beginning of trade.)

The powerful city of Troy situated at the entrance of

the Black Sea controlled the trade since they could either let the ships pass or not. They collected stiff fees for passage and grew rich. So about 1200 B.C. the Achaeans, who were growing increasingly strong, saw no reason they should not save the fees. They invaded Asia Minor, laid siege to Troy and destroyed it.

About this siege, the minstrels made up stories, added fantastic details about gods, and piled on dramatic improvements until we now have the Troy legend. Homer (or various poets whom we now lump under his name) collected the pieces in 850 B.C. and made the poems out of it that still survive today.

Despite all the fantasy contained in the legend, it still depicts the life of the Mycenean Age fairly accurately. For instance, the heroes used bronze armor and swords, since the use of iron for weapons had not yet developed.

But let's turn to the legend of Troy, rather than to the real history. It is the legend that has added words and left traces in our language; while as for the real history, about that we still know very little.

The legend begins with a beautiful Nereid named *Thetis* (thee'tis). (She has a place in the heavens, since the seventeenth planetoid to be discovered was named "Thetis.")

She was so beautiful that both Zeus and Poseidon were in love with her. However, the Fates (or perhaps the wise Titan, Prometheus) warned Zeus that Thetis was fated to have a child far more powerful than his father. This meant that no god could marry her since her child would then overthrow Zeus as Zeus had overthrown Cronus and Cronus had overthrown Uranus. In order to prevent that from happening, it was decided to marry Thetis to an ordinary mortal.

The mortal chosen was *Peleus* (pee'lyoos), who had been one of the Argonauts. Peleus was the son of *Aeacus* (ee'uh-kus) who was the son of Zeus. The jealous Hera hated Aeacus and sent plagues to Aeacus' kingdom that destroyed almost every man there. Zeus, in pity, changed ants into men that repopulated the city. For that reason, the subjects of Aeacus and of his son, Peleus, were called

Myrmidons (mur'mi-donz), from a Greek word meaning "ant."

The Myrmidons were excellent soldiers and fought at the Trojan War. They kept antlike qualities of obedience and discipline. Even now, we still call professional soldiers who will fight ruthlessly for anyone who will pay them "myrmidons."

The occasion of the wedding between Peleus and Thetis was a time of great celebration and merrymaking. All the gods attended except *Eris* ("ee'-ris"), the goddess of discord, who had accidentally been overlooked. She appeared suddenly and tossed an apple into the crowd which rolled to where Hera, Athena and Aphrodite were standing in conversation.

On the apple was inscribed in golden letters "For the Fairest," and of course the question arose as to which goddess was most beautiful. Hera, Athena and Aphrodite all claimed the apple and not one would allow either of the other two to have it. Nor was any god brave enough to make a decision in the matter. (Because of this portion of the legend, any object over which people or groups of people quarrel can be called an "apple of discord.")

The only thing to do was to put it up to some mortal whose judgment the goddesses would agree to accept. The choice fell on a young shepherd named Paris, and with him, the city of Troy enters the story.

According to legend, the region of Asia Minor in which Troy was located was originally colonized by a group of men from Crete. This is probably correct, since Troy, most likely, was under Minoan rule to begin with.

One of the early kings was *Dardanus* (dar'duh-nus), from whom the land was named Dardania and who founded a city named Dardanus. This city existed on the shore through much later times and from it came the modern name "Dardanelles" for the strait which had been earlier called the Hellespont.

(Dardanus was a son of *Electra,* one of the Pleiades, and this is sometimes said to be the Lost Pleiad. She is supposed to have dimmed her light rather than witness the destruction of Troy.)

Later kings included *Tros* (one of whose sons was Ganymede, whom Zeus carried to heaven) and *Ilos*. Both founded towns which eventually joined to form the city of the legend. From the former, the city was called "Troy" and from the latter "Ilium."

Both names are used in the legend. For instance, Homer's poem about the siege of Troy is called the *Iliad* meaning "about Ilium." Since the *Iliad* has a great deal of suffering and bloodshed in it, the word has come to be used humorously (but only rarely) to mean any long hard-luck story.

The son of Ilus was *Laomedon* (lay-om′e-don), who was king of Troy in the time of Heracles. Heracles, on a trip to Troy, saved *Hesione* (he-sie′o-nee), the daughter of Laomedon, from a sea monster, as Perseus had saved Andromeda. When Laomedon went back on his word and refused the reward he had promised, Heracles and the men with him attacked Troy, captured it, killed Laomedon and put Laomedon's son, *Priam* (prie′am), on the throne. Moreover, they carried off Hesione a captive. It was Priam who was king of Troy at the time of the Greek siege.

Priam married *Hecabe* (hek′uh-bee) and other women and had a total of fifty sons and twelve daughters. Hecabe is better known under the Latin version of her name, *Hecuba* (hek′yoo-buh′).

Priam's oldest son was *Hector*, who was the chief warrior on the Trojan side. He was the underdog at all times, fighting a stronger army with steady bravery. In fact, the Trojans as a whole were greatly admired for having held off stronger forces for ten years. The phrase "to work like a Trojan" or "to fight like a Trojan" means to work or fight with great industry and endurance.

Yet although Hector has always been considered a model patriot, his name has come to mean "to bully" or "to threaten." To be sure, Hector makes boastful speeches in the *Iliad,* but so did all the heroes. It was customary for them to do so.

Another of Priam's sons was *Paris*. Before Paris was born, Hecabe dreamed that the child she was going to have turned out to be a burning brand. An oracle assured her this meant that the child would be the cause of the burning and ruin of Troy. Consequently, Priam and she decided to have the child killed. They entrusted the task to a herdsman, who couldn't bring himself to kill the pretty child. Instead, he left him exposed on a mountainside expecting him to die. However, Paris was found by shepherds and raised as one.

It was to this Paris that the goddesses came for a decision as to which was to get the apple of discord.

The goddesses each tried to bribe him. Hera offered him riches and Athena offered him fame as a warrior. Aphrodite, however, offered him the most beautiful woman in the world as his wife. Now Aphrodite, as the goddess of beauty, was the most beautiful of the three in any fair competition, so that when Paris gave her the apple it was a good judgment. However, Hera and Athena were bitterly offended, and from then on they were deadly enemies of Paris and of Troy.

After that, Paris visited Troy where he was victorious in various athletic events. He was recognized as the long-lost son of Priam by a rattle that had been exposed with him and that he still kept as a souvenir of his childhood.

However, Priam had a daughter named Cassandra (kuh-san'druh) to whom Apollo had given the gift of prophecy. Later, Apollo grew displeased with her, and spoiled the gift by arranging it so that although she always prophesied the truth, no one would ever believe her. When Paris was taken back into Priam's family, she prophesied wildly that he would bring about the ruin of Troy, but no one believed her.

Nowadays, any person who prophesies doom and evil is called a "Cassandra," particularly if his warnings seem exaggerated and are not believed. The most famous Cassandra of modern times was Winston Churchill. During the 1930's he constantly warned against the dangers of Nazi Germany and was not believed.

Meanwhile, Aphrodite had to fulfill her promise to Paris. At the time, the most beautiful woman in the world was Helen of Sparta, the daughter of Leda and the sister of Castor and Polydeuces. When the time came for Helen to marry, every hero in Greece was anxious to take her as wife, so great was her beauty.

Her father, *Tyndareus* (tin-day'ree-us), King of Sparta, was afraid to give her to any one of them, lest the rest make war on him in revenge. He therefore called the heroes together and got them to agree to let Helen make her own choice and to promise that thereafter each would defend whoever was chosen against all enemies.

Helen chose *Menelaus* (men'e-lay'us), who was the younger brother of *Agamemnon* (ag'a-mem'non), the king of Mycenae and the most powerful ruler in Greece. Menelaus, along with Helen, received the throne of Sparta and became king. As for Agamemnon, he married Clytemnestra, the sister of Helen.

It was Helen, then, whom Aphrodite decided to give to Paris for a wife. Paris arrived at Sparta as a visiting prince. (Cassandra warned this would be a fatal voyage but no one listened to her.) Paris was feasted and treated with every courtesy. However, Aphrodite caused Helen to fall in love with him and to join him when he left for Troy.

There she stayed throughout the war and has ever since been called "Helen of Troy." Like Aphrodite, she has been the model of beauty ever since.

The memory of Helen as the most beautiful woman who ever lived shows itself in the fact that it is still a popular name. In ancient times, names taken from the myths were very commonly given to youngsters. Once Christianity took over, however, names were chosen from the Bible instead and from the saints. The Greek myths weren't considered proper to use in naming children.

Only a few names from the myths survived this change in fashion and those were mostly girl's names. Examples are Irene, Cynthia, Phoebe, Diana, Flora, Iris, and Grace. An example of a boy's name that comes from the myths is Jason.

But the only name from Greek mythology that has always remained extremely popular through all of Europe and America ever since Greek times has been Helen. It has taken different forms such as Helena, Ellen, Elena, Elaine, Eleanor, Eleanora, Ella, to say nothing of pet versions like Nellie and Nell. It is not easy, after all, to forget the most beautiful woman who ever lived and the one, as we shall soon see, who caused the most famous war of all time.

Finding his wife gone, Menelaus sent messengers to all ᵖᵃʳᵗˢ of Greece reminding the various heroes of their ᵖʳᵒᵐise and requesting all of them to join him in an ᵉˣᵖᵉdition against Troy to get Helen back. First, ambassadors were sent to Troy demanding the return of Helen. Priam refused on the grounds that the Greeks still kept Hesione, his sister, whom Heracles had carried off.

That meant war.

Not all the heroes were willing to go. One, who was very reluctant to do so, was *Odysseus* (oh-dis'-yoos), King of the island of Ithaca. He is better known by the Latin version of his name, *Ulysses.* Odysseus had married *Penelope,* a cousin of Helen, and had just had a little son named *Telemachus* (te-lem'a-kus). Naturally, he did not want to leave his family.

However, Odysseus was famous for his intelligence and shrewdness and the Greeks felt they had to have him. He feigned madness but they were able to penetrate the pretense and forced him to stick to his oath.

It was also foretold by soothsayers that the Greeks could not win unless they had the help of *Achilles* (a-kil'eez), the son of Peleus and Thetis. (It seems strange that all this started at the wedding of Peleus and Thetis and that already they had a son of fighting age. What is worse is that before the Trojan War was over, a son of Achilles had reached fighting age. However, the myth-makers never counted the years too closely.)

It was Achilles who, as the son of Thetis, was destined to be far more powerful than his father. And he was, for next to Heracles he was the most famous of all Greek heroes. Moreover, the victories of Heracles were achieved through sheer superhuman strength. Achilles, while exceedingly strong, was pictured as a skillful fighter, not someone who simply laid about with a club.

When Achilles was born, Thetis tried to make him immortal by dipping him in the river Styx. She held him by one heel as she did this and forgot to dip him a second time in order to get the heel wet, too. The place where she held him therefore remained untouched by the water of the Styx and that part remained mortal. As a result, during the Trojan War, he was finally killed by an arrow in the heel, the one place where he could be mortally wounded.

For this reason, any weak point in an otherwise solid defense is called an "Achilles heel." Furthermore, the strong tendon that connects the muscles of the calf of the leg with the heel bone is called the "Achilles tendon."

Thetis knew that Achilles had a choice of two fates. He could either stay at home and lead a long, quiet life, or he could join the Greek forces and die young, but gain eternal fame. Thetis would rather he lived long so she dressed him as a girl and hid him on the island of Scyros with other girls.

Hearing rumors of this, Odysseus and a Greek delegation traveled to Scyros and here the wit of Odysseus began to pay dividends. It would have been unmannerly to search the girls. Instead, Odysseus brought presents of clothes and jewelry for the women but included a sword as well. The various girls seized upon the pretty presents, but one girl couldn't resist seizing the sword and swinging it forcefully to test its balance. That girl, of course, was no girl at all, but Achilles, and so he joined the Greek forces. With him went his best friend, *Patroclus* (pa-tro′klus), plus a group of Peleus' army, the Myrmidons.

Achilles proved to be the greatest of the Greek warriors and any great warrior may now be called an Achilles. For instance, the Duke of Wellington, who defeated Napoleon at Waterloo, was at one time called the "Achilles of England." Similarly, any crafty man may be called an "Odysseus."

Many of the Greek heroes who joined the forces were sons of Argonauts. Achilles was the son of the Argonaut Peleus, and Odysseus was the son of the Argonaut *Laertes*. In addition, two heroes named *Ajax* (ay′jaks) joined. ("Ajax" is actually the Roman spelling of the name, the Greek version being *Aias*, pronounced "ay′as.")

One was a huge, strong man, the son of the Argonaut *Telamon* (tel'a-mon) and usually called Ajax the Greater. The other was the son of the Argonaut *Oileus* (oh-i'lyoos) and was usually called Ajax the Lesser. *Diomedes* (die'o-mee'deez), the son of the Argonaut *Tydeus* (ti'dyoos), also joined and proved one of the major heroes.

Even Crete was still powerful enough to send an important hero, *Idomeneus* (eye-dom'en-nyoos).

One of the heroes was actually a veteran of the hunt of the Calydonian boar. This was *Nestor,* king of the city of Pylus. He was an old man at the time of the Trojan War (probably sixty, which was extremely old in an age when the average man was dead at thirty). He survived the war too and lived on at least ten years beyond it, so that he must have been at least in his eighties when he died. He is pictured in the legends as a man of wisdom and experience whose advice was always good, so that a "Nestor" has come to mean any wise old man.

On the whole, only heroes are mentioned in the Troy legend but one or two minor characters have left traces in the language. At one point, Homer mentions *Stentor* (sten'ter) as a herald who was useful at rallying the army because he had a voice as loud as fifty men.

For this reason, anything loud is said to be "stentorian" and the howling monkey whose resonant bellow can be heard at a distance of a mile or more is sometimes called "Stentor." The same name is given to certain one-celled creatures which make no noise at all, you may be sure, but which are shaped like megaphones which, of course, are associated with noise.

Again, Homer pictures *Thersites* (ther-sie'teez), the one commoner mentioned in the *Iliad,* as being an ugly, cowardly agitator always spewing curses at the heroes. Actually, the one speech Homer gives him is full of good sense, but the poems were usually sung to an aristocratic audience, so Thersites was made fun of. Poets other than Homer introduced Thersites as an offensive insulter and now "thersitical" has come to mean "loud-mouthed" or "scurrilous."

The various heroes, or at least some of them, on both

sides of the Trojan War, are to be found in the heavens. In 1906, the German astronomer Max Wolf discovered a planetoid that was unusually far from the sun. The path it followed did not lie between that of Mars and Jupiter but seemed to be nearly identical with the path of Jupiter. This was an unusual orbit for a planetoid and such planetoids, as I explained before, received masculine names. Wolf called it "Achilles."

If a line is drawn from Achilles to Jupiter, then to the sun, then back to Achilles, it forms an equilateral triangle (that is, a triangle in which the three sides are all equal). Astronomers know that such a situation is stable. That is, a small body equally distant from two large ones would always move in such a way as to remain equally distant from them. As Jupiter moves about the sun, Achilles moves with it, keeping almost exact step.

That same year another planetoid was discovered in Jupiter's orbit, and in 1907 two more were discovered. Then still others. Some of them were discovered in a cluster with Achilles and some were discovered on the other side of Jupiter, forming a second equilateral triangle with Jupiter and the sun. "Achilles" set the precedent and the rest of these planetoids were named after heroes of the Trojon War. The second to be discovered was "Patroclus," on the other side. Others followed on both sides. Along with Achilles are "Antilochus," "Diomedes," "Odysseus," "Agamemnon," "Menelaus," "Nestor," "Ajax," and "Hector." Since all these but Hector are Greeks, these are referred to as the "Greek camp." Along with Patroculus are "Anchises," "Troilus," "Aeneas," and "Priamus." Since all of these but Patroculus are Trojans, this is the "Trojan camp."

As a group, the members of both camps are called the "Trojan planetoids." Furthermore, the situation where a small body is equidistant from two larger bodies is now called the "Trojan situation." So far, no case is known other than the one involving these planetoids.

The Greek army assembled at Aulis, a seaport near Thebes, and prepared to sail. However, matters began badly. There was no wind.

A soothsayer told Agamemnon that the wind would rise only if he sacrificed his most beautiful daughter to Artemis. Agamemnon therefore sent a lying message to his wife, Clytemnestra, asking her to send him his daughter *Iphigeneia* (if'i-ji-nee'uh) in order that he might marry her to Achilles. When his daughter arrived, he sacrificed her and the wind rose promptly.

However, Clytemnestra hated her husband bitterly from that moment.

When the Greek army finally reached Troy, they settled down to a long siege. The Trojans stayed behind their walls, which were too strong to be assaulted. The Greeks raided up and down the coasts, trying to starve out the Trojans. For nine years, there was a stalemate.

Homer's *Iliad* begins its famous story in the ninth year of the siege. The key event in the plot was a quarrel between Achilles and Agamemnon, over the division of some of the spoils of war.

As a result of the quarrel, Achilles in anger withdrew himself, together with Patroclus and the Myrmidons, from the war. He remained in his tent and refused to fight. Moreover he asked his mother, Thetis, to persuade Zeus to bring defeat upon the Greeks so that they would have to come begging to him for his help and thus soothe his ill-temper.

Thereafter, the Trojans emerged from their city and under the leadership of Hector began to drive the Greeks back, while Achilles smiled. As a result, anyone who abandons a fight because of hurt feelings, and lets his comrades down, is said to "sulk like Achilles in his tent."

The Greeks eventually sent to Achilles to beg him to return to the fight, but he refused. The Greeks were driven back to their very ships and were faced with utter defeat. Then Patroclus, Achilles' friend, filled with pity, begged permission of Achilles to put on Achilles' armor and fight in his place. Achilles gave the permission and Patroclus led the Myrmidons out to battle.

For a while, Patroclus drove back the Trojans who at first thought it was Achilles coming back to fight. Achilles had, however, warned Patroclus to do no more than drive the Trojans back from the ships and on no account to attack Hector. Patroclus, enchanted by his own success, felt that not even Hector could stand against him. (There was hubris again.) He charged Hector and was killed (nemesis, of course).

At once, Achilles was filled with rage and despair. He would have charged immediately into the fight but he had no armor. He made friends with Agamemnon rapidly, got a new set of arms (forged by Hephaestus himself) from Thetis, and then leaped into battle.

He drove the Trojans before him like sheep and all of them fled behind the walls of Troy. Only Hector remained outside, ashamed to flee, and determined to fight Achilles and die, if necessary. The two met in a duel which (as told by Homer) is one of the greatest scenes in all literature, and Hector was killed.

Shortly thereafter, Achilles was killed by an arrow in the heel from the bow of Paris.

Two of the Greek heroes competed for the honor of possessing the armor of the dead Achilles. These were Odysseus and Ajax the Greater, each of whom claimed to have done more for the Greek cause. The Greeks voted the armor to Odysseus, and Ajax the Greater killed himself in despair.

Even with their two greatest champions dead, the Greeks fought on. As for the Trojans, Hector was dead, and Paris soon died as the result of an arrow from the bow of *Philoctetes* (fil'ok-tee'teez) who had inherited Heracles' poisoned arrows. He had been left behind when the Greeks sailed for Troy because of a wound he suffered, but he rejoined the Greek forces after Achilles died.

But even with Paris dead, the war did not end. Helen was simply married to another son of Priam, *Deiphobus* (dee-if'o-bus), and the war went on.

An oracle then suggested that Troy could not be captured as long as the Palladium (a statue or bust of Pallas) remained within its walls. (I've mentioned the Palladium earlier in the book.) Diomedes and Odysseus entered Troy in disguise and stole the Palladium, but still Troy did not fall. Achilles' son, *Neoptolemus* (nee'op-tol'e-mus), who was also called *Pyrrhus* (pir'us), now joined the forces and the Greeks were much heartened, for he seemed so like Achilles that they felt their great champion had come back to life.

But still Troy did not fall.

It was then that Odysseus had the great inspiration of the war. He suggested that the Greeks build a huge, hollow horse, capable of holding armed men inside it. The Greeks were then to leave this horse standing on the field outside Troy and to fill it with armed men, while all the remaining Greek warriors were to get into their ships and sail away just beyond the next cape where they would lie hidden.

This they did. The Trojans saw the Greeks leave and were puzzled by the horse. A Greek named *Sinon* (sié-non), left behind, pretended to be a deserter from the Greek forces. He said the Greeks, in despair, had decided they would never conquer Troy and had sailed for home. The horse was an image dedicated to Athena and if the Trojans took it into the city, Athena would see to it that the city would never fall to any enemy.

The Trojans gave themselves up to wild joy and set about bringing the horse into the city. They even broke down a portion of the walls to make an opening large enough.

A Trojan priest of Apollo, named *Laocoön* (lay-ok'oh-on), was the only Trojan to warn against this. He said, "I fear the Greeks, even when they come bearing gifts." (This has become a proverbial phrase meaning that one must not trust a long-time enemy even when he suddenly begins to seem friendly.) However, Poseidon, who was on the side of the Greeks, sent a serpent out of the sea to kill him and the Trojans therefore felt sure that Laocoön was wrong.

They brought the horse into the city and that night when the Trojans were sleeping after a day of gaiety, the trap door opened and the Greek warriors came out. They set fire to the city and began a slaughter, while the Greek fleet which had been hiding just out of sight returned.

Neoptolemus killed the youngest surviving son of Priam and then Priam himself. Menelaus was going to kill Helen, but when he saw her beauty he could not do it and took her back. The only important Trojan to escape was a relative of Priam's family, named *Aeneas* (ee-nee'us). According to later Roman legends, his descendants founded the city of Rome.

As a result of this part of the Troy legend, any group that worms its way into the heart of enemy country and waits for a strategic moment to strike is called a "Trojan horse." The most famous recent example was that of certain internal traitors in Western countries during World War II.

When the Trojan War was over, the various Greek warriors who survived made their way home. For the most part they did so only with great difficulty, suffering shipwrecks and misfortunes. Agamemnon was killed the first day he arrived back in Mycenae by order of his wife, Clytemnestra, who had not forgiven him the sacrifice of Iphigeneia.

As for Menelaus, he and Helen wandered for seven years before finding their way back to Sparta. Much of the time was spent in Egypt waiting for a favorable wind to carry them back to Greece. While there, his steersman, *Canopus* (ka-no'pus), died and his name was given to the brightest star in the constellation "Argo." Thus a steersman was fittingly placed in a ship.

The star Canopus is the second brightest star in the sky but is located so far south in the heavens that it is never visible in Greece (or in New York for that matter). It is just visible in Egypt, however, far down on the southern horizon so that the Greeks might well imagine it to represent a mythical character who died in Egypt rather than in Greece. (Actually, there was an ancient Egyptian city named Canopus and the star may be named for that.)

At last, Menelaus captured a sea god named *Proteus* (pro'tyoos) who, he was told, could tell him how to get back to Greece. Proteus had the power of changing shapes and in an effort to escape changed into a lion, a serpent, a panther, a boar, running water and a tree. However, Menelaus held fast throughout and Proteus was finally forced to explain the exact sacrifices that would bring on a fair wind. Menelaus followed orders and finally got back to Sparta, where he and Helen ruled peacefully thereafter.

"Proteus" is a name now applied to anything that changes its shape such as the one-celled animal called the amoeba. Anyone who changes his mind or his opinions easily, to suit circumstances, is said to be "protean."

Of all the heroes, however, the one with the longest and most famous homeward journey is Odysseus. Homer's second long poem describes it.

The poem, almost as great as the *Iliad* (and even more popular), is Homer's *Odyssey*. Any long and complicated journey is now called an "odyssey."

Odysseus' ten-year wanderings all over the Mediterranean are filled with fantasies and fairy tales. One of his first stops was at a land where the inhabitants ate a fruit named the lotus. Anyone eating it forgot everything but the pleasure of eating it and wished only to stay in that land forever. Some of Odysseus' men ate of the lotus and had to be forced back to the ships by the rest. For that reason, anyone who lives in ease and luxury and gives no thought to duty is called a "lotus-eater." The plant itself is completely mythical, of course, but its name has been given to various water lilies.

Odysseus and his men next came to an island on which dwelt huge Cyclops. One of them, a man-eating monster named *Polyphemus* (pol'ee-fee'mus), captured Odysseus and twelve of his men, brought them to his cave and began to eat them, two at a meal. Odysseus tricked the Cyclops into drinking wine and getting drunk. While the Cyclops was sleeping, Odysseus succeeded in putting out his eye. He then tied his men to the bottom of the sheep of Polyphemus' flock. The blind Cyclops let the sheep pass while waiting at the cave opening for the men, and so they escaped.

Because of the fame of this story, a "polypheme" is sometimes used to mean a giant and one very large moth has been given the name of "Polyphemus moth."

Polyphemus was a son of Poseidon and after that, Poseidon was always sending storms after Odysseus. Finally, Odysseus reached an island on which lived *Aeolus* (ee'o-lus) god of the winds. Aeolus gave him a bag filled with all the winds but the west wind. If Odysseus kept the bag tightly closed, only the west wind would blow and that would bring him home to Ithaca.

They were within sight of Ithaca and could even see the smoke of burning fires on the shore when the exhausted Odysseus fell asleep. His men, also tired, thought the mysterious bag (which somehow they could not believe contained nothing but wind) might contain wine. They opened it and, at once, all the winds flew out and in the storm that followed, the ships were driven far off to sea, hopelessly lost.

There is reference to Aeolus in several words. An "aeolian harp," for instance, is an arrangement of strings which will hum with soft tones when the wind blows through it. Sand carried by the wind is called "aeolian sand." There is even a word "aeolistic" which is used to describe talk that is full of "hot air."

Aeolus was considered the father of the winds, each of which was a different demigod. *Boreas* (boh'ree-as) was the rough north wind and our word "boreal" means "north" in consequence. The kindest of the winds was the west wind to the Greeks. It did not bring cold from the north or heat from the southern deserts but blew gently and mildly. The Greek name for the west wind was *Zephyrus* (zef'i-rus) and now any gentle, mild breeze is called a "zephyr."

Odysseus next underwent a disastrous meeting with another set of man-eating giants, the *Laestrygones* (lestrig'o-neez) who destroyed all but one of Odysseus' ships.

Odysseus and his one remaining ship came to an island called Aeaea (ee-ee'uh) on which lived a beautiful enchantress named *Circe* (sur'see) who was the daughter of Helios. She could change men into animals, apparently for amusement, and changed Odysseus' men into pigs. (As a result, anything which seems pleasant but which has the power to make men behave like beasts, as liquor will, for instance, is called "Circean.")

Odysseus himself was immune to Circe's spells because Hermes had brought him a flower called "moly" which would give him protection when he smelled it. The plant is entirely mythical but the name has been given to certain plants of the garlic family. (It is true that a garlic odor may keep beautiful women from trying to enchant you.)

Odysseus forced Circe to change his men back into their natural shape and then stayed a period of time on the island, as a pleasant rest from his voyages.

Eventually, he felt he had to try to get home again and, on Circe's advice, he traveled to Hades to get the advice of a dead soothsayer on how best to do this. (It was a favorite device of the mythmakers to have their heroes visit Hades. Theseus, Orpheus and Heracles had all visited Hades.)

After accomplishing that successfully, Odysseus sailed past the Sirens. He protected his men by having their ears filled with wax so that they could not hear the Siren song. He himself listened to it but had his men tie him to the mast first and made them promise not to release him however hard he begged. And though he did beg, they did not release him.

One of the Sirens, named *Parthenope* (par-then'o-pee), was so upset at this failure to trap the shrewd Odysseus that she threw herself into the sea to her death. She was washed ashore at the city of Naples, which was therefore sometimes called "Parthenope" by ancient poets. The name cropped up again in modern times. In 1799, French troops captured Naples and established a republic. It only lasted a few months, but while it did it was called the "Parthenopean Republic."

Having left the Sirens, Odysseus had next to pass between two cliffs. On one cliff, there lurked a monster called *Scylla* (sil'uh), another of the children of Echidna. She had a human body out of which grew six long necks at the end of each of which was a yapping dog's head. Below the other cliff was a monstrous daughter of Gaea called *Charybdis* (ka-rib'dis). Three times a day she sucked in water, making a terrible whirlpool that would destroy anything trapped in it.

Odysseus had to decide near which cliff to pass. Ever since, any choice that must be made between two dangers equally bad is said to put someone "between Scylla and Charybdis." (Scylla and Charybdis are assumed to have been located in the narrow Strait of Messina that separates Sicily and Italy. Of course no monsters exist there, though there is a whirlpool of a sort. Still, a rock on the Italian side is called "Scylla" even now, while one on the Sicilian side is called "Charybdis.")

Getting back to Odysseus— He decided that rather than risk losing the entire ship to Charybdis, he would run the gantlet of Scylla. In doing so, he lost six men, one to each set of jaws of the dog-headed monster.

He then landed on the island of the sun, where Helios kept herds of cattle (the "cattle of the sun"). Circe had warned him not to eat these, but as they were becalmed and time passed, the crew grew desperate with hunger and against Odysseus' orders killed and ate. Consequently, when the ship finally set sail again, Poseidon had full permission to raise a storm that destroyed the last ship. Only Odysseus himself, who had not eaten of the cattle, survived.

Alone and adrift, Odysseus was cast ashore on the island of Ogygia (oh-ji'jee-uh) where a nymph, *Calypso* (ka-lip'so), kept him prisoner for seven years. He was so homesick, however, that finally Calypso agreed to let him go. He built a raft which carried him to the land of the Phaeacians (fee-ay'shunz). These were skilled sailors and they brought him back to Ithaca at last.

On Ithaca he landed as the only survivor of all those who had left with him for Troy twenty years before and had left Troy for home with him ten years before.

During the lapse of time before Odysseus' return, the rumor had naturally spread in Ithaca that he was dead. Over a hundred noblemen of the island and surrounding territories therefore tried to persuade Penelope to marry one of them, in order that that one might become the new king.

Penelope put them off because she was faithful to Odysseus who, she was certain, was still alive and would someday return. (Her name is used today as the model of a modest and faithful wife, just as Clytemnestra's name is used as the model of an unfaithful one.)

Penelope had to resort to tricks. For instance, she explained she would have to weave a shroud for Odysseus' old father, Laertes, before she could marry anyone. This job she began, but each night she would unravel whatever she had done during the day. For that reason any job which seems never to get done is called a "web of Penelope." ("Web" of course, means "something that is wov   ")

F a'ly, the trick was revealed to the suitors by a disloyal maid and they grew threatening indeed. Odysseus' young son, Telemachus, was, of course, the actual heir to the throne, but he was powerless. The only one he had to help him was an old adviser left behind by Odysseus. This old adviser was named *Mentor* and "mentor" now means any adviser or counselor. "Monitor," meaning the same, or someone whose job it is to warn of approaching danger, is another form of the word.

Telemachus, fearing he would be killed and seeing no way out of his troubles unless Odysseus came home, decided, on the advice of Mentor, to visit some of his father's old friends to see if they had news of him. He visited Sparta, where he met Menelaus and Helen, now safely back from their own wanderings. He also visited Nestor, who was still alive, though older than ever, and who was the only one of all the Greeks who had returned home without trouble.

However, there was no news of Odysseus, and he returned home downhearted. Yet the trip had served the purpose of keeping him away during a period when the suitors planned to murder him and by the time he was back, Odysseus had landed.

Odysseus was fed and treated well by *Eumaeus* (yoo-mee'us), a goodhearted swineherd who did not recognize him. Odysseus dressed as a beggar and mingled with the servants in the halls where the suitors feasted in order to see how matters stood.

By this time, Penelope had been forced to the end of her trickery, so she agreed to marry whichever suitor could draw Odysseus' old bow and shoot an arrow accurately at a mark with it. (She could only hope that none of the suitors could match Odysseus' heroic strength.)

To be sure, each suitor failed to pull the bow. The supposed beggar (who had by now revealed himself to Eumaeus and Telemachus) asked the chance to try and, as a joke, was allowed to do so. He drew the bow easily, whereupon he and Telemachus, together with Eumeaus and a few other faithful servants, caught the suitors by surprise and killed every one of them.

Odysseus and Penelope were reunited at last. Odysseus' old father, Laertes, helped make peace with the fathers of the suitors and the *Odyssey* comes to an end.

EPILOGUE

THERE ARE some legends concerning the days after the Trojan War and of the sons of the heroes of that war. The most famous involve *Orestes* (o-res′teez), the son of Agamemnon, who avenged his father by killing his mother, Clytemnestra. For this crime, he was hounded by the Erinnyes (or Furies) until he was purified in Athens.

Hermione (her-mie′o-nee), the daughter and only child of Menelaus and Helen, first married Neoptolemus, the son of Achilles, and, after his death, she married Orestes. To round things off, Telemachus, the son of Odysseus, married Circe, the enchantress his father once knew.

The Achaean kingdoms, however, came to an end within a century of the Trojan War, when there was a new invasion by an uncivilized set of Greeks who till then had lived to the north of Greece.

This new invasion was by a group of Greeks called the *Dorians* who, about 1100 B.C., destroyed Mycenae and Tiryns and established themselves permanently in various parts of Greece. The Dorians had iron weapons, and the Achaeans, with bronze weapons only, which were neither as tough nor as strong, could not stand up against them.

In the legends, the Greeks described the Dorians as coming into Greece under the leadership of the descendants of Heracles. The sons of Heracles ("Heraclids") had been driven out of Greece, but their grandsons returned, defeated the son of Orestes and conquered all the lands they claimed were Heracles' by right of conquest.

In order to explain how the Dorians came to take over all the cities they did take over, later mythmakers made up tales which had Heracles conquering a large number of different cities.

Some Achaeans remained, notably the Athenians. Others fled to Asia Minor, where they established many Greek cities which for a couple of centuries were more civilized than Greece itself which, under the Dorians, passed through a barbarous period.

However, once the Dorians conquered Greece, the age of legend was really over. The golden blaze of fantasy and fairy tales, of gods and heroes and monsters gradually died away and the flat daylight of ordinary history slowly dawned.

And yet the Bronze Age did not die altogether for it left behind it a never-to-be-forgotten heritage of stories, which remain part of our literature and life. Even if it ever happened that no one read the stories, our English language would still contain within its words the memory of those days of gods and heroes.

GENERAL INDEX

MYTHOLOGICAL INDEX